HOW TO BE HAPPY

How To Be Happy

JOHN PEPPER

GATEWAY BOOKS, BATH

Published in 1992 by
GATEWAY BOOKS
The Hollies, Wellow,
Bath, BA2 8QJ

Reprinted 1995

First Published 1985
by Routledge & Kegan Paul

Cover Painting by Zampighi: 'Sweet Music'
Designed by Studio B of Bristol

Set in Sabon 10½ on 11½ pt
Printed and bound by
Redwood Books of Trowbridge

A catalogue record for this book is
available from the British Library

ISBN 0 946551 79 0

Man is not born for happiness
Samuel Johnson

We're born to be happy, all of us
Alfred Sutro

Contents

Introduction:
H.H. The Dalai Lama

In his book, *How To Be Happy*, John Pepper presents the meaning of happiness and ways to achieve it in a manner that is easy to understand and free from any particular cultural bias.

The question, how to achieve happiness, is crucial to all of us. All sentient beings from the tiniest insects to the most powerful human beings are the same in wanting happiness and not wanting suffering. Moreover, all have an equal right to achieve happiness and eliminate suffering.

Now, in order to achieve happiness it is important first to identify suffering and its causes, because from certain points of view happiness is the state of being free from suffering. However, we must approach this with patience; it is not something that happens all at once. In our ordinary pursuit of happiness we require food, clothing and shelter to provide simple physical comfort. But this of itself is not a guarantee of happiness, for even wealthy, healthy and strong people can be unhappy. What we need is a combination of physical and mental happiness. Of the two, it is mental happiness that is more effective. Therefore, we should emphasize ways of bringing about a happy mind.

One way of doing this is to try to manage our thoughts and mental attitudes. The more we indulge in such negative attitudes as anger, desire, pride and jealousy, the more we act on them, and, because they tend to fuel conflict, frustration and insecurity, the more unhappiness we create for ourselves. However, if we actively cultivate a more positive outlook based on the fundamental human qualities of love and compassion, we will be able to counteract our negative feelings and bring about peace of mind.

The author writes that happiness is a state of mind or being, a kind of energy, which can help us to overcome defeat and transcend pain. Its very foundation is love, a sense of care and concern, not as an occasional remedial exercise or philosophical ideal, but as a way of relating to the world twenty-four hours a day. Although the world cannot be changed overnight, by paying as much attention to our inner development as to our external circumstances, we can lay the foundations for both ourselves and others to be happy.

November 26, 1991

Prologue: Hard Times

All of us want to be happy, but looking around us, at the lives of our friends and acquaintances and even of those we are prone to envying, the rich and famous, most of us encounter all too little happiness, all too much sorrow.

The terrible things that have happened on our planet this century have brought us to the threshold today of scenarios such as the·advent of the world of Orwell's *1984*, collapse of international order, and nuclear tragedy. As a result, the prospect of any individual finding happiness appears more remote now than ever. Indeed there are those who argue that we have come to live in such an horrendous age that the very idea of individual happiness in it is impossible, or tantamount to an obscenity.

They say: how on earth can we be 'happy' in the midst of such suffering? Is not the pursuit of our own happiness the biggest 'Me' or ego trip of all?

The trouble with this line of argument is that if pain and misery are deemed the only realistic or respectable responses to what is happening in the world, how do we keep alive the qualities – of love, joy and humour – needed to build a better one? To counteract doom with gloom only creates a dead-end for all of us.

In contrast, it is good perhaps to recall the example of those who survived, with their minds and spirit intact, the worst that the twentieth century has thrown at us so far, the horrors of the Nazi death camps. These stalwarts did so only by keeping alive, in the core of their ravaged bodies, the flames of the human will to happiness even in the throes of the most unthinkable tragedy.

The greater obscenity, surely, is to meet darkness with its own kind? At a time of such widespread unhappiness, if we care about what is happening, is it not our duty to discover if it

1

might be possible to be happy as individuals and, if so, to learn how to share that happiness with others?

All the majority of us can do, we who haunt no corridors of power, only our fears, is to try to make the world a slightly better, happier, place for our being in it.

This then is a book about happiness and how to find it – or rather, how to let it find you. It is above all a simple book. This is because the essence of its subject matter is simplicity. There is nothing complicated at all about the art of living happily, which is why, in a world that has tangled itself in such dreadful knots, we find happiness so elusive.

It is more than anything a book about love, because the simplicity at the root of happiness is only discovered when we care sufficiently about others and the world in which we live to refrain from the worst games, the wheeling and dealing, that go with excess of ego and always end up complicating things so much. It is about a species of love as quiet and unassuming but as sure of its goal as thistledown sailing on the breeze.

It is a very different kind of love from the one being touted not so long ago as the cure-all for our ills, in the so-called Sexual Revolution. To the extent that there is today less prudery and perhaps a little more honesty in the sexual climate, we could be said to have gained something from it. But it seems that in the end we may have progressed only from one sexual dark age to another; from the hypocritical, reaching its peak in the Victorian era, to the mechanical, reaching its peak, in its obsession with orgasm and performance, in our own. In addition, licence seems to have led directly to ever-increasing disease. Altogether, sex as a new religion has come to fail us as much as the old.

The love we are concerned with here, as a way of life, is not, either, of the Elysian variety purveyed by drugs or the worship of gurus. Such may have afforded a few individuals insight into unusual levels of consciousness, but the prospect of universal rapture appears, now, to have passed us by.

So, finally, standing today among the ruins of faith, politics, lust and 'bliss', fundamentally as unliberated as we ever were, we hover on the brink, it appears, of global despair.

Our brief for the future looks clear, therefore. Either we begin to enter a new age pretty quickly, in which 'love-making' extends way beyond mere sexual activity and becomes a way of looking at the world and acting accordingly, so we attempt to 'make love' of everything we say and do (even indeed of our copious failures to do so), or we perish.

In other words, we have to progress urgently to some new sort of spiritual base for our lives else the misery being felt across the planet will surely reach a level where large sections of the population begin, if subconsciously, to look upon the oblivion (perhaps) of Armageddon as a relief, and in the process contribute to its encroachment.

The spiritual base alluded to here is not foreseen as any mass return to the somewhat dog-eared formalities of church or temple. Instead, it is perceived as a dramatic quickening of the survival instinct which occurs normally when the life of any individual or species is threatened, propelling it into radical new ways of behaving (adapting) if the threat is to be overcome – and logically the only saving alternative for a world in which ignorance, greed and hatred have brought it to the brink of self-destruction is one instead in which the counter-values of understanding, selflessness and love prevail, and do so on an appreciable scale, with dogma or ideology of no importance any longer. Literally, if we are to have a future, there has to be a change of heart.

This is a book, therefore, about changing your own. A start.

Of course, since the fabrics of all our lives are very different from one another's, I cannot tell you *precisely* what you must do to find happiness. All I can do (as others have done and continue to do, against all the odds sometimes, for myself) is point in the general direction. The journey itself, with all its stops, starts and detours – and, I would add, its excitements – you must make alone.

The hour is late. *Bon voyage.*

Chapter 1
Waking up

There is no such thing as happiness as it is popularly understood and pined for.

The notion of it as a sort of hoopla prize whereby we shall come to be spared conflict, pain, doubt and the thousand and one other things that go to make life such an obstacle course for most of us, is about as realistic a picture as expecting Father Christmas to chair peacekeeping talks between the Irish.

Life is and, so far as we can see, always will to a considerable extent be about conflict, pain, doubt and so on, and the only way we can effectively escape these unpopular interlopers is to give up the ghost on life altogether. Believers in divine judgments or reincarnation will argue of course that we cannot flee them even then.

So, realistically, our search for happiness cannot concern itself with flights from misfortune. Essentially it must concern itself with facing it, coping with it and finally making something encouraging of the result. At this point some people, peering down a long dark tunnel of one disappointment after another until the day they die, may decide that happiness of any kind is not possible in this life, that where it does advertise itself it is only illusion.

These are the Wounded of the Earth, the teeming legions of them. Perhaps they are right, and the happy and the righteous are self-deluded. I don't know.

All I do know is that what happiness I have experienced is a very pleasant self-delusion if it is one, far more enjoyable and creative than the reality of my unhappiness and bad behaviour, and that the only life I can see worth the living as an individual is one where the good things turn out to be as 'real' as the bad ones, and where each reconciles itself to the other. This seems to me to be the recipe for a reality grounded even today in peace.

A lot of us are bitter, perhaps beyond recall. But I think it is safe to say, in view of the fact that the world is still vaguely in one piece and that the mass of mankind continues to go about its business, finding something in life that makes it worth its while, that the majority of us, battered though we may be, are sufficiently *compos mentis* and open to life to know in our bones that happiness is more than a myth.

This majority, this teeming majority, is still able to respond with feelings of joy to a rainbow, the sound of a soft wind in the leaves of a tree, or, if we are particularly fortunate, to the light in the eyes of those we care for. And these are feelings, wrenching also out of the depths of our being, which are surely every bit as real as the pain and confusion.

For practical purposes therefore, from now on we will take happiness as a reality. Our task is to try to find a way of living in which it can grow even when it has to share house-room within ourselves with endless . . . pain and confusion. At the moment there is too much of the latter in our lives; far too much. Unhappiness has no problem flourishing, it grows like weeds. We have to find ways of giving the tender plant of happiness an equal chance.

Accepting, realistically, that our existences are never likely to be beds of roses, we see that happiness will have to come from finding a practical solution to the all-pervading problem of unhappiness, a solution indeed to that which we cannot solve, namely the mystery of life. The accent is on the word 'practical'. Happiness has to be woven into the warp and woof of one's life as it is lived else it is only so much theory, and as we know from experience, our own and history's, mere theorists – dreamers, philosophers and the like – have rarely been noted for their peace of mind.

If happiness is to grow within us it has to learn to withstand the assaults of external circumstances. It has to be a state of mind, of being – an energy – which enables us to defeat defeat, and transcend pain.

A happiness that only arises when circumstances are favourable and promptly vanishes when they are not, cannot be seen to offer much of a solution to one's problems in an age so riddled with them. Happiness susceptible to the whims of fortune can hardly be described as the genuine article, and it is the genuine article we are after.

A happiness that is proof against misfortune, the only happiness worth the name, has to be built of course on formidable foundations.

Now for many this base will be a formal religious one, still, entailing a belief in a God or gods who might or might not be seen as architects of misfortune but who will certainly offer the believer a way of handling it, a 'meaning' for it that spares the collapse of his world into chaos. Such belief, enabling the adherent to withstand the slights of this life with a pinch of salt since he is certain there is a solver of riddles and redeemer of ills in one to come, is a valuable asset, understandably, in any quest for happiness.

However, it possesses one serious design flaw. If our belief comes at any time to falter, or crash altogether, as belief is not unknown to do when confronted with some of misfortune's darkest deeds, our happiness is certain to sway or nosedive with it.

There are those of us then who want to base our happiness on something even stronger than religious belief; on an *absolute certainty*.

However, since the only two certainties the present life appears to offer are those of uncertainty and death, the thought of neither of which exactly endears itself to most of us, we might appear to be whistling into the wind at this point. Basing our happiness on (a) the fact that we can rely on nothing, and (b) the fact we are going to die a death which might amount to 'nothing' – it seems to be asking a lot of us, does it not?

If we think about it a moment though, it does not seem such a bad idea at least, after all. If we can find ways of being happy that are so self-contained, so independent of circumstances, that nothing we add to or subtract from the life giving room to the happiness can diminish it, this happiness we have found is a very precious thing indeed.

It is a happiness founded on nothing except itself. It is not something tied with a cord or teat, for sustenance, to something outside itself. If we prove to ourselves that happiness is possible and sustainable without 'belief', the happiness is secured in a knowledge gained from direct experience. We deal in fact, not faith. And what we know to be true from experience is something that can never be taken away from us.

Such truths are our only safe possessions in a shifting world.

A happiness based on 'nothing' – no political ideology, religious doctrine, material possession, or relationship – is in the end the only kind that is shockproof.

As for the common species of alleged happiness based on wealth and power, leaning heavily on other people, or on ideas – alas, the susceptibility of props like these to change, their insecurity, makes for a decidedly fragile product.

To find the sort of happiness that survives chaos and to understand what it consists of, we have to do a lot of testing on the way. We have to find out for ourselves what does and does not work, and discard the latter.

It is rather like panning for gold, in a way. There is a lot of digging and sifting to be done before we can hope to get sight of what is of value. There are many errors to be made and usually much suffering to be experienced. Then there is no guarantee anywhere that we will strike lucky anyway. The only thing that keeps us going is our unhappiness; what more poetically has been called our 'divine discontent'. We are simply fed up with pain.

We have to learn the hard way because it seems human beings cannot learn efficiently by any other. It is usually pointless telling a bubbling twenty-year-old on the threshold of a brilliant career, for instance, that money has nothing to do with happiness. To him, with the world at his feet, it is so much theory again, or a bleat of pure pique or resentment. Through disappointment and tribulation, suffering, he has to learn the truth of the observation for himself. Then he can begin to look for other sources of his happiness.

It takes most of us a very long time to work through the rubbish. If someone is on the dole and depressed, try telling him, too, that money has nothing to do with happiness. 'Disappointment and tribulation' here do not appear to be making any more contribution to the stock of wisdom than does the cockiness of the youth with his tail up!

Then what about those who have 'made it'? As we get older we might well get increasingly disenchanted with 'making it'; with jobs, nice homes, marriage, good times, travel, going to church on Sundays or meditating in lotus positions as potential foundations of our contentment. We might make one or two pretty brave attempts to change course altogether, do things with our lives that startle our friends, neighbours and even ourselves. But the waves of sleep that beat upon our sensibilities in a weary world frequently ensure we get washed back to the point we started from.

And not surprisingly, a lot of folk give in. We cannot summon the energy to fight any more. It is all too much for us. Happiness, the real commodity as distinct from the counterfeit, proves as elusive as ever. Whether we are rich or poor, there seems no way we can win.

However, it is at the point of throwing in the towel, of coming to be pretty fed up with everything, that interesting things *can* occur.

Now we have stopped chasing fantasies, it is possible for us to start seeing things as they really are. A certain cool clarity invades our perception. We note the games, lies and futilities around us. We tot up all the energy we have expended, all the hurt we have come by, in having spent our lives in that round. It is a relief to know we do not have to do any more looking in *that* direction. A large chunk of our lives can drop away now like dead wood. And, accordingly, it happens sometimes that we do experience a strange new feeling here of lightness, peace.

Desperation, the feeling we have come to the end of the road, can be a singularly important landmark in the journey to happiness. Of course it may prove quite a terrifying experience, but just as childbirth can be painful, sometimes unutterably so, so too is the giving birth to a mature adult.

For maturity means giving up the infantile pursuit, in search of happiness, of the daft things we get addicted to from the start; and as we know, the symptoms of withdrawal from any addiction can be lacerating. We also know, however, that they are an indication of a return to health.

If, when it seems we have come to the end of our tethers in the quest for happiness, we can stand back a moment and understand that our misery is only a grieving for the loss of a way of life that is familiar but which would itself go on causing us misery if we were to continue hanging on to it, we can begin to see our stupidity, even laugh at ourselves, and feel a bit better.

It can even begin to feel good to realize one has burned all one's bridges – that there is no going back. The unknown, the future with no shape or certainty, can prove a tremendous excitement as well as a terror. Loss, anguish, are able to breach whole reservoirs of stagnant energy within us and give an entirely fresh momentum to our lives. Hence the sayings 'Every cloud has a silver lining', and 'Sweet are the uses of adversity'. Despair, even though it may feel like it at the time, does not have to be the end of the world. Seen for what it is, and used skilfully, it can be precisely what we need to build a new one.

All right, you say sceptically, if nothing really makes us happy any more, yet real happiness has to be founded on 'nothing', how do we make the connection? Surely we have to work with *something*?

How do we begin?

Ask yourself what makes you happy. If you do have the essentials of food, clothing and shelter taken care of (and if you have not, one would agree that happiness might prove a little more difficult to attain, though not necessarily so, as we shall see later), what is it you want in your life more than anything else?

Is not the answer something on the lines of being able to love and be loved, to have the peace and security of kinships with your fellow men based on mutual support and affection? There might be a few of us, strays of one kind or another, who live for other things – finding God or Understanding by going off to the desert, dedicating our days to the pursuit of some rare or esoteric knowledge, or winning power over people; the sort of single-minded ambition which is prepared to sacrifice familiar bonds with others. But I think it fair to say that most of us yearn more than anything else for a relationship, relationships, of human love.

Of course most of us want more than this to complete the sort of happiness we have in mind.

We want some kind of public recognition as individuals, an assurance we are esteemed for our character and skills; for what we are. We want work that is enjoyable and of value to self and community, and pays us enough to spare us any worries about survival. We want to feel we belong in a community. We want to have fun and leisure. We long to have some sort of purpose in our lives so that they might rise above being mere existences.

All these and more are traditionally seen as important contributions to an individual's wellbeing. But first of all, the bedrock of everything, what we want is love.

We do not always know by any means what we mean by the word, which is an indictment in itself of the thousands of years of our history in which it has been bandied about so freely and used, as a promise of happiness, to jail people more often than free them. Love is as natural, as indispensable to life as breathing, and for us to be reduced to saying 'I'm not so sure I know what love is', as the state of our world would suggest rather a lot of us have been, and our soul-searching would corroborate, is a measure of the disaster that hangs over us.

Looking at the brighter side, however, the fact that most of us still hunger instinctively for love as overwhelmingly the most important ingredient in a life worth the name, even though we are not always sure what it might amount to at its more rarefied levels of expression, offers us ground for hope. Mankind remains capable of being deeply moved by simple acts of kindness, by our ability to reach out to one another instead of clawing at one another. We still know tears of shared sorrow, and what it is to care.

As the millennium arrives it may be that our follies will catch up with us, that we shall know a breakdown in civilization of a severity hitherto unknown, as many a portent suggests. But what we can never destroy altogether, as we can observe from the story of all creation, is the impetus to something better; in human terms, the will even in our darkest hour to create a community in which you and I are able to be open and tender with each other, deeply conscious of our common humanity and all its ills, and compassionate as a result, no matter who we might be or whence we came. It may be that our own evolution as a species is taking us to the point where nearly all the cultural props and possessions most of us have always believed to be an indispensable part of happiness will be destroyed, leaving us with the one ingredient we truly need, the sorrow that leads to the compassion that leads to love.

As we stand, we live in an age that is itself adolescent, our

lives self-centred and grasping and full of confusion and
squalls. Its collapse might be the beginning of our social
maturity. The imperative of the present time is to try if we can
to avoid the terrible connection, and make a bid for that
maturity without the collapse.

Our search for happiness therefore is essentially a search for
love, of a kind that will free us from the variety that has
become mere lip service and an instrument of exchange and
mart, and as a result been the prime responsibility for the
disillusionment lying at the heart of our unhappiness as
individuals and the parlous state of the institutions through
which we live as social beings.

It is a search for a species of love which will enable us to be
in touch with happiness even if we have not got a job or
partner, a colour television or a 'do' booked for Saturday night.
The sort of love for life in general, for ourselves and all men,
even though we might not believe remotely in God or gods,
which can have us crying out in the midst of our worst
misfortunes, 'Rain or wrack, I shall not crack!'

We look for the strength to be able to withstand what . . . all
right, all that the rest of this benighted century might heap
upon our heads, and to begin with, the strength to haul
ourselves out of our present doldrums; the strength to *dare*.

Most of us are cowards. We cower behind masks. We live by
roles. We hide under stones instead of exploring the stars. We
keep compromising and being bought out and sat on. We learn,
usually long before we even reach middle age, how to die in our
shoes; conform. We become grey people with grey thoughts in
a grey world.

This way it is admittedly possible we shall get worn into the
sort of groove where, being exposed neither to the extremes of
ecstasy nor terror, we find a muffled, plodding acceptance of
life, a certain guiding stoicism. But we shall be lucky if we do.

The truth is that most of us will get so bored, so fed up with
living in bodies from which all intensity of feeling has been
drained, we shall want to scream. And if we cannot scream, as it
is the polite thing not to do in a grey world, it is likely we shall
turn to alcohol, drugs, adultery or blacking the wife's eye
simply in order to find (albeit in a roundabout, unfortunate
way) this lost, lamented world of feeling. If we are ever to

know real happiness, this is a world we have to rediscover in some way or another. We have to climb out of our ruts.

No, this does not mean we have to pack our jobs in, get a divorce, sell the house and head for Timbuktoo (though some people might find it helpful). It means that in the ordinary course of our days we have to be prepared to make ourselves vulnerable, step into the unknown, and take risks more. It means we have to have the courage to let ourselves be hurt, to admit that one has made something of a pig's ear of one's life and to say to oneself, with a deep determination to turn the pig's ear into a silk purse, 'Enough's enough!'

We might be afraid at this stage. But after the long years of hibernation in a routine that has closed our pores, jaded our palates and put scales in our eyes, that decision, 'Things are going to change', and the fear it arouses in us, do at least (at last) make us feel alive.

Already, quite an accomplishment.

Chapter 2
First setbacks, first secret

One thing that can be almost guaranteed to follow that wonderful ringing declaration of 'I'm going to be happy come what may', within a few days if not hours, is an onslaught of depression. We crash before we have even set off. We feel almost foolish. One moment we are feeling so exhilarated, taking off for the moon like that; next we are back where we started, if not farther back, bluer than ever.

However, we all know what we are like when it comes to doing anything that involves serious change in our lives. It's hard. Very. And time and again we get nowhere, we go round and round on the same old treadmill. We are slaves of ourselves, of habit. It seems there is no way out.

Instead of getting fed up and angry with ourselves, however, which only adds to the weight of failure, it would be more useful if we stopped a moment, acknowledged this fact, and decided instead to be a little gentler on ourselves. So we failed: so what? What is so special about failing? Do not millions of us, all of us, go on failing in one thing or another from one day to the next, all through our lives?

'The sorrow that leads to the compassion that leads to the love that leads to happiness' – it is a causal chain we would do well to keep fresh in our minds at every stage of the journey. If we are going to have to learn how to extend real compassion to others we will never be able to do so until such time as we can show such compassion to ourselves. So when we are down in spirit we should try to be as easy on ourselves as we aspire to be, one hopes, with friends and neighbours when they are under the weather.

If we get irritated or worse by our own failures we would have to betray a certain schizophrenia not to be affected similarly by the failures of others, no matter how much we might hide the fact under public words of condolence and

13

support. Charity, therefore, begins at home in more ways than one.

Important to remember too is the sheer scale of the enterprise before us.

Normally when we make resolutions about improving ourselves in one way or another we have a precise idea of what we need to do. To improve our health we give up cigarettes. To get a better job I have to go to night school and get some fresh qualifications. To save his shaky marriage William must learn to do something with his temper. And so on. All these tasks are not easy.

The nicotine habit is usually tenacious; having to study at night after a day's work can be too much for many; and dealing constructively with anger can be as nerve-racking a business as handling unexploded bombs. But at least we can spy a target for our endeavour and a way of aiming for it.

In this case, however, looking for happiness, we are in essence searching for a meaning in life, and there is no pursuit more grand or audacious, or one that has seen more people flounder and perish on the way, or above all one whose quarry is so defined in whispers and beheld through so much fog.

So we should not be in the least surprised to find ourselves, a lot of the time, and particularly at the start, wandering everywhere and nowhere. In the modern world the shout, for everything, is 'I want it now!' With regard to our enterprise this is unfortunate. For a start, happiness, as we shall come to see, is never won by 'wanting' it overmuch, by grabbing at it. And second, even if we have stopped 'wanting' and learned instead that we must 'want for nothing' in the final analysis to get within sight of our goal, it might still take us a lifetime or longer to behold it in its entirety.

It is meet therefore that we have patience and be gentle with ourselves.

That said, the prospect of a lifetime going nowhere in our search for happiness, of falling short of the goal like a parched straggler chasing a mirage in the desert, is not calculated to do very much to lift one's gloom, I admit. It seems an enormous investment of time and energy in an enormous risk.

It is.

On the other hand what is the alternative? Settling for the

bankrupt routines and ideologies that have left you feeling so desperate finally that you have even been driven (a little guiltily perhaps, like someone tiptoeing through the Lonely Hearts columns) to burrow for crumbs in a book like this?

No, there is no way back. We have had our fill of living death. The road ahead, wherever and to whatever it might lead, is the only tenable direction.

That's the bad news out of the way. Now for the good news. All of us, every single one of us, is happy already. Truly!

The staggering fact is that in the search for happiness the goal lies right under our noses. There are no far-flung journeys to go on, though we shall almost certainly have to venture on any number before we get sufficiently exhausted to realize the fact. And it is possible to begin to experience an ever-ripening happiness, and one doing so at quite a rate of knots, from the moment we do start to realize that on all these journeys we are like someone racing towards his destiny with one foot nailed to the floor-boards.

Once we fully accept that there is no one or no place 'out there' that can provide our happiness, it is possible, having been suicidal at dusk, to know peace by dawn. Wherever we are, whatever we are doing, the prize is there for the taking – now, or never. It is just a matter of seeing.

Now if you happen to be skimming through this nonsense whilst you are standing in the dole queue in the rain, with a nice hole in your boot and the wife on the run with an Italian hairdresser, to be informed that, whether you care to agree with the fact or not, 'You are happy already', might appear an impertinence of a high order on the author's part.

But what I mean when I say we are happy already is that each of us, unable to have our happiness given us by anyone else or come from anywhere else, therefore contains both the seed and the womb together of our own happiness.

It is not coincidence that when our lives change course altogether and we undergo psychological renewal, we are said to be 'reborn'. When we were born the first time (in this life at least), we had external parents. Our parents now are simply *the opposite halves of ourselves* which up to now have caused us so much unhappiness through their unremitting conflict, but which have finally come together in reconciliation and peace.

Happiness is merely wholeness. Sadness is 'split'.

Our being able to be reborn therefore is dependent on a process of love-making, of opening ourselves up to love, in the depths of our psyches. Somehow we have to impregnate ourselves, with something. How? with what? we wonder.

Let us accept that our happiness will have to depend on love of some kind – a love leaning on nothing, a love that 'just is'. A love, remember, tied to no creed, ideology, possession or relationship . . . something, some inner knowledge, feeling – a way of looking at the world and working with it – that will enable us to survive any pain or hardship. Think about it a moment.

It is quite a goal to aim for, seemingly quite a distant one too for most of us, is it not? A matter of our being able to love a good deal better than we do right now?

But with all this business of a 'psychological love-making', of 'impregnating ourselves' in the first place with 'the seed of a happiness we possess already', it appears, does it not, that we are being asked to 'love a good deal better than we do' . . . *right now*? In short the destination is the journey?

Precisely.

But how can we love properly and be happy, now, when the blatant fact is we do not know how to love properly, how to be happy? It doesn't add up!

Many of us are familiar no doubt with the limpid and almost haunting Chinese proverb, A journey of a thousand miles must begin with a single step, and understand its importance. In our journey for fulfilment it is important, yes, to start as we intend or would like to finish. Since love at a level all of us can understand is to do with simple tenderness and kindness, these are the simple qualities we decide to start cultivating from the beginning. We will quietly nurture them in ourselves and try to use them as our fundamental currency with others.

What we do is make a quiet commitment to try and cherish this worn old globe and its inhabitants a little more, to work not for our own personal happiness particularly but for that of Spaceship Earth. We impregnate ourselves, if you like, with this vow on behalf of others. Concern is our 'seed'. Our 'womb' is our consciousness on all its levels, our whole being, in which we are going to try and give birth to ourselves as new selves.

This essentially private act becomes linked now to a public goal.

It's not just a 'Me' trip after all.

So while of course the commencement of any enterprise such as this will not in all probability match in quality, remotely, the kind of goal we have in our mind's eye, it is nevertheless vital to ensure that end and means are at least broadly in sympathy with each other. If they are not, we are in danger of falling into the trap that has snared millions of people, indeed entire nations and political creeds, this century; those prepared to use any means to a desired end; to murder, incarcerate and torture – reduce continents to rubble – in the name of a 'better world'.

Today we have begun to understand the folly of an advocacy of love-and-brotherhood via a process of Big Brotherhood and hate. It is, as Jung has taught us, the advocacy of those who are so 'split' themselves they know fundamentally nothing but despair; nothing whatever about the rudiments of happiness, the laws of life. We do not find happiness making others unhappy. The acorn begets the oak, not the willow.

To start as we would finish, then (to die wise and happy, perhaps we would agree?), is a matter almost of assuming we are wise and happy already, and acting accordingly. It is not, however, a case of pulling the wool over our eyes. Nor is it one of gritting our teeth and play-acting in public, pretending to care for others and be happy when the truth is we hate their guts and generally feel downright miserable, as is rather more likely to be the case. Wisdom is simply awareness, and this is something we can foster from the beginning.

We can acknowledge bluntly to ourselves that we do not love this or that person and that we do feel unhappy, and then we can go on to ask ourselves, equally bluntly, *why*? Happiness begins with the self-inquest that leads to self-knowledge. For the inquest to be, to do, any good, it has to be ruthless. At this stage, naturally, one or two (if not three or four) of the answers are still likely to be less than ruthlessly honest. It does not matter. To be completely honest with ourselves we would have to be sages, and we are a long way short of that.

We are, however, beginning the long, usually painful, but sometimes exhilarating process of finding out who we are and why we act the way we do. We have to find out what it is in us that makes us so unhappy.

However, while we undergo this reflection we still have to go on relating directly to those we dislike and to the unhappiness we feel, and the division we experience at this stage between examination and action can make us feel unequivocally schizophrenic sometimes. This is normal and nothing to worry about.

How, you insist though, should one 'act' here? How can I love somebody while they continue to stick in my craw?

Not an easy one, this. Certainly we should not feign an excess of brotherly love to hide our negative feelings. One of the sickliest sights in the world is the forced smile of the spiritual trouper who is 'trying to be nice' whilst a quiet hate or resentment gnaws away in his heart. He is all grimace. What we can do at this point is endeavour to ensure our negative feelings do not run away with us, that we retain a measure of control. A control, however, that is not something rigid (like the plastic spiritual *bonhomie*), but a degree of detachment, an acceptance of our hostility as something real but ultimately of no great importance.

We can also remember, perhaps, what the psychologists tell us – about our disliking most in others what essentially we dislike most in ourselves: the problem of projection. In effect, in this business of getting to know ourselves better, our so-called enemies, acting as mirrors to the worst in us, can become our greatest 'friends'!

Here we have a case then where instead of shying away from people or circumstances we do not like, we can even welcome the dislike and the discomfort, since they are telling us important things about ourselves and why we are unhappy. We attempt to turn a negative situation into something positive. Now we relate to the person we do not particularly care for with a little more neutrality and quiet curiosity than we have summoned in the past.

It is a fact that most of us spend our lives striving to secure the things we like, and rejecting those we do not. We have a very definite idea of what will make us happy if only we can organize it, i.e. bring together all the desirable ingredients. But these desirable ingredients have an uncanny knack of course of never quite coming together at the same time, so we find we are never quite happy.

E.g.: we have the job and the home we want but we would like to have the ideal lover to complete the picture, or we have a job and a nice relationship but my partner and I are looking for the ideal love-nest. And all the time we are living for the future that will be our 'happiness' when all the pieces fit in the puzzle.

But when we have got the job, home and relationship we have sought – the Big Three most of us are after, let's face it – and are sitting back congratulating ourselves on our good fortune, how do we cope then with sudden redundancy, being forced to move elsewhere, or our other half falling in love with someone else? The answer is we don't cope. We collapse. Our happiness bursts like a bubble.

By believing happiness consists only of the good things, we are in fact doomed to a never-ending unhappiness. Of our setbacks and sorrows, the bad things, do we eventually fashion our deepest joys.

In trying to reconcile the opposite halves of ourselves which are at war and cause us so much trouble, so we attempt to reconcile the good fortune and adversity that weave in and out of each other constantly through all our days. The two tasks are one.

As we saw at the beginning of chapter 1, instead of running away from misfortune from now on, trying to create an unreal world which will be free of it, we have to accept that it has to be integrated somehow into our happiness every bit as much as the enjoyable things that happen to us.

And if this is the case, surely we can start looking at the painful things, as with our 'enemies', in a new and more hopeful light?

Since our setbacks cannot be wished away, they are *here* – but somehow they hold the key, the mystery, to our happiness – perhaps we can start feeling a little inquisitive, even benevolent about them, even while they are causing us so much hurt? Instead of screaming 'Why the hell does this have to happen to *me*!' when something dreadful occurs, perhaps we can mutter 'OK, what the hell can I do with it now that it *has*?'

Finding happiness, we see, is a relentlessly practical, down-to-earth affair. It is not a magical mystery tour.

Once we have begun to get into a frame of mind which sees that everything we do, everything that happens to us – literally everything – is valuable stuff, an entire lesson in itself in our training ourselves to be happy, we begin automatically to react less violently to the 'slings and arrows of outrageous fortune' anyway. Right from the start we have opened up the possibility of a little more happiness and a little less pain in our lives simply by becoming more accepting, or philosophical.

Happiness, we perceive more and more, is nothing to do with outside circumstances. It is only a state of mind.

This or that is happening to you right now, causing upset: so, pause, go and have a cup of tea, or go and break a few plates and scream (repressing anger is never healthy); but once you have got yourself into a reasonable state where there is no more flame belching from your nostrils, ask yourself *why* this is happening to you, and then (even if you don't come up with an answer) *what can I do about it?*

This is the self-inquest leading to the self-knowledge we have been talking about; the point where we start making some sense of our confusion – the beginning of happiness.

I think we shall find that if we are honest with ourselves, the reason we feel sick to death when disaster strikes is based on two things.

First it involves the collapse of our wishes, our plans. I wanted this and instead I got that. I feel thwarted, frustrated. Downright mad. My scheme of things has been wrecked. 'I', 'I', 'my' – it is an affront to our egotism.

Second, disaster often means the collapse of our being able to make sense of anything. Our idea of who we are, what we are doing – indeed our idea of what life 'is all about' – becomes utterly meaningless.

My child gets run over in the road: how can I believe now in a 'benevolent God'? Time and again good people seem to fare worse than the less deserving, so how does this square with what we are taught about the 'natural laws of justice'? I see civilized values collapsing everywhere under the onslaught of barbaric ones, so what is the point of trying to be 'civilized'?

Altogether . . . why *bother?*

Our unhappiness then is to do with the world not coming up to our expectations of it, both in so far as our own lives and those of others are concerned. From the onset of my being able to shape a view of the world, at a tender age, I expected happiness as an individual and I reckoned on a society in which others would find it too. And I expected the sum of the parts, life in general, to 'make sense'. Clearly our unhappiness has something very deeply to do with 'expectations'; hopes that let us down.

From which we might deduce that our happiness has something to do therefore with having none?

This, ancient wisdom has always had it, is so.

But, you protest, how can one possibly live in a world where one has no expectations? If we don't look to the future and plan ... dream ... how on earth can we evolve, construct a civilization? If we had no expectations would we be any better off than beasts? Is it not our capacity to reflect and imagine, to envision a future, what separates us as humans from them?

The trouble is, we confuse creativity with expectations, and tend to ruin the former with the latter.

Man creates his unique world because he cannot help doing otherwise; his ideas are part and parcel of his being man. And as all of us know, it is the act of being creative, of *act*ually drawing up the blueprint for a better tomorrow, of gardening, decorating a room or sitting down with a friend and helping her sort out a problem, which can be one of the deepest wellsprings of what happiness we do experience in life.

It is the one hundred per cent involvement in what we do that gives us that warm feeling of fulfilment.

Unrest on the other hand comes from wishing we were someone else doing something else, somewhere else. It comes from not being in the moment.

If we draw up that world blueprint simply in the hope of winning some recognition and power for ourselves in the future, do the gardening because we want to compete with the horticultural prowess of the neighbours, decorate a room solely because we hope to save money by doing the job ourselves, or try to help our friend because it might in some way be to our advantage eventually, we are looking for something other than experience of the act itself; we are not wholly involved in it.

And because we are not wholly involved, and because it is quite likely we shall not get what we hope for anyway out of our divided attentions, we are never going to enjoy the experience simply *for itself*.

Similarly with doing the things we do not enjoy doing: because we expect them to be boring, irritating and so on, we ensure they are. To add expectation to action is to reduce its potency, its capacity to surprise and teach us things.

Expectations either reducing us to dark mutterings or lifting us into roseate dreams together deny us the living-in-the-present which offers our only hope of real happiness. Necessity and choice can be strange bedfellows therefore – impediments on our journey. To be happy we cannot be other than where we are.

Of course, planning an economy or a new town to take people away from slums, or writing a book about happiness which you like to think may help a few people, are the sort of things human beings do do in creating their unique world, so in one sense we are looking to the future and having hopes of what our current decisions and actions might achieve, all the time. Our restlessness, our spur. And it is of course perfectly true that an economist, town planner or writer can add to the apparent sum of human happiness without, indeed, being happy himself, in which case there appears a strong argument here for saying to hell with the individual's needs, let us get on with the community's.

However, the happiness offered by the economist, town planner or whatever can only be received if we as individuals are capable of receiving it; of being sufficiently open to it. A sizable tax rebate born of some splendid fiscal juggling, a nice new home in a quiet street as a result of an imaginative rehousing programme, or a bit of inspiration and food for thought from a printed page are in themselves, obviously, not the slightest guarantee of *your* happiness.

In short, forward-thinking offering a theoretical improvement in the human condition does not necessarily bring about any real advance in happiness either for the forward-thinker or the beneficiary of his gifts. The political and social utopianism we have witnessed this century in particular is a graphically cruel illustration of the incapacity in themselves of either politics or society to provide us with the happiness we seem to crave as individuals. It seems that in the end it is something we have to find on our own.

All right, you say; so I'm unhappy and this is probably a lot to do with my having too much concern for myself and too many expectations in life and not being able to live in the fabled 'here and now', and maybe in a world as torn as it is the only way I can stop being torn is, somehow, to heal myself. I can make vows, try to turn over a new leaf; care for others a little more. I can try to be more detached from my sorrows.

But the truth of the matter is, right now, I am as unhappy as ever. I'm stuck. And so, miserably (desperately) you repeat, *what can I do about it?*

The secret, really, lies in doing nothing at all.

Chapter 3
Letting go

The sad, simple fact is most of us try too hard, too hard by half, to be happy.

Instead of seeking to learn how to live wisely, we demand to know how we can be 'glad', 'turned on'. And as we observed in passing in the last chapter, these days not only do we want happiness and all we like to think goes with it, we want it *now*! We believe we have an inalienable, constitutional right to happiness no matter what. In the age of fast-this and instant-that, when the ideal we are supposed to envy is 'life in the fast lane', it is not surprising that we expect to have our personal happiness on tap, too.

There exists however a very old, wise saying which has been lost sight of in the stampede for satisfaction, and which we would do well to ponder. Namely that happiness is never found by those who look for it. Or, as Chuang Tzu put it, 'Perfect happiness is the absence of striving for happiness.'

The modern age led us to believe once (and not all that long ago) that all we had to do was will something to happen and, lo and behold, the miracle of science and technology would sooner or later, and preferably sooner, come up with our heart's desire. Science was God. One of the reasons for the present psychological depression everywhere is our growing up to realize that science has its limitations like the rest of us and the fact that it has taught us a way of relating to the world, a materialistic one, which cannot cope with a reality denied these materials. Chastened by events, we might be starting now to accept the improbability of jam tomorrow, of a future of anything other than bread, but what makes us particularly miserable is the fact that most of us are now programmed to want and expect jam, and especially 'jam today'. We do not know what simplicity is. So we go on craving and hurting.

As happiness retreats further and further – whether 'things'

are taken away from us or whether they pile up in greater
profusion does not matter – our desperation grows. In the
former instance we will almost certainly try harder than ever to
get more 'things' to prop up our tottering 'happiness' even
though they get harder and harder to come by. In the latter
instance we might do the same or, sated with 'things', try all
the harder to find happiness through excess in other quarters –
sex, drugs, gambling; anything to try and put that edge back on
one's ever-diminishing senses.

Whatever; like something trapped in a web we struggle. And
tangle the more.

To get out of this terrible mesh in which most of us find
ourselves it is obvious we shall have to do something very
different from the kind of things that have got us into it. The
same old patterns have produced the same old disappointments,
even the same old disasters.

What is needed is radical change.

But because of our conditioning, 'radical change' often
amounts to very little change at all. On the surface it might
seem that we are embarking on all kinds of weird and
wonderful ventures to haul ourselves out of our mess. We
might give up our job in the Civil Service and go and stay in an
Indian ashram, or finally enter therapy of some kind, or
emigrate with the family to the other side of the world to try
and start all over again. We could give up cigarettes and booze.
We might throw ourselves into voluntary work for the needy,
the sick. . . .

All of these are possibly very commendable, useful changes
of direction. They might illustrate courage and imagination,
even oblige us with an early, perhaps unprecedented experience
of fulfilment, even joy. After all the 'blahs' one has endured in
life, sudden surgery can be quite a rousing business. It can also
be a seductive one on a mass scale: in the last twenty years,
'radical change' has reached crisis proportions – every other
person it seems is doing something dramatic now to try and
alter his or her life. So finally all bodes well, you may think.
Looking around however, can we truthfully say it does?

Hasn't the Counterculture itself, by and large, only come up
with an alternative despair?

Whichever way we have approached the finding of our

happiness, whether from an angle 'straight' or 'hip', the trouble has been that we have *tried* too hard.

All the time, we are trying to manipulate circumstances to our advantage. If this direction does not come up with what I want, let's try that one; and failing that, a third. Even if I do pitch into the effort of trying to care more for others, at the back of my mind there is the old hope lurking around, that somewhere in all this there might be something in it for me.

I may not want to be rich and famous any more but in my resignation to poverty and anonymity I am certainly hoping for no end of unworldly compensations. Even if I do not aspire either to wealth or beatitude, if I just want to be left quietly on my own, no ambitions of any kind, I am aspiring not to aspire! I am still looking for *something*. I have a rough draft of the sort of life I think I would find appealing.

What is unfortunate about this 'perfectly natural' way of behaving is that we get very attached to its ideas and designs. They take us over, they 'become' our lives. So when our plans have to be modified drastically as they come up against brick walls or get dashed altogether on them, our lives naturally buckle or break in the process.

What we lack is a life free of wanting and striving that can go on being itself, not reacting overmuch to external events, keeping us on the level, when the wanting and striving let us down. We need a space, a centre, within ourselves which is impervious to attack – a sort of psychological air-raid shelter. As things stand we are so in thrall to *what happens to us* that we cannot really be said to be free individuals at all. We are at the beck and call of fate, and this can become a very confusing, tiring affair.

What we seek therefore is, on the one hand, the energy and imagination that will enable us to make constructive choices in our lives and, on the other, an inner freedom that will spare our getting hooked on them and hurt when they disappoint, as they will, time and again, inevitably; an inner freedom that will prevent our getting too wrapped up in our own ambitions, and so keep altruism alive.

If we have tried too hard to find our happiness, looking for it everywhere except the place where it is, within ourselves, and only made ourselves unhappy in the exercise, it makes sense now, if we are still determined to find an answer somehow, to try to do just the opposite, which is in effect to 'un-try', to stop working so hard at our happiness. This is the *really* radical approach to the problem after a lifetime going round in circles and getting tied up in knots. We have to learn how to stay still. How to let go.

And of course, we must not in the process try too hard to 'un-try' or let go, either. . . .

But here, very simply, is the first secret of happiness – the little shrug that doesn't say 'To hell with it', but the opposite; saying, 'The pain I'm suffering doesn't really matter one iota in the cosmic scheme of things, so let's address this one small life to the latter.' It is the shrug not of no-concern but of the laying aside of self-concern, and this is the first principle of the kind of love we have lost sight of in our frenzied search for it.

Admittedly after a lifetime of twitching and grabbing, with the universe generally in orbit around oneself, it is considerably easier to understand the good sense of the proposition than it is to put it into practice. A few of you, lucky souls, might be so deeply impressed by sudden confrontation with it in all its glorious simplicity, its absurd obviousness that nevertheless defeats the understanding of entire civilizations (so-called), that your lives will be changed dramatically in the moment . . . 'My God, there is nothing to *do!*'

For most of us however it will not be like that at all. We shall put as much effort into letting go of things as we did into hanging on to them, and we shall go on extracting as much frustration, failure, as of yore. The task of getting rid of the idea of a task is not going to be an easy one.

On the encouraging side, however, 'letting go' can have some very early results, perhaps small but quite identifiable ones, which are sufficiently interesting and even stimulating to make you realize you are not altogether chasing a dead horse. You get a taste of possibilities. You want to go on.

Very quietly, a relationship might start improving. You could find yourself sleeping better, laughing a little more. You might find work less of a chore. Your mind, your view of the world, might feel it has shifted its position half an inch; you see things a little differently, as if you are looking out on a parched landscape which is suddenly refreshed by a shower.

For the first time in a long time you might be able to feel the rousing power of your heartbeat, a taste of excitement ('I've stopped being stagnant, I've started moving!') on the back of the tongue. It is indeed a delight, a blessing, not to be dead in your shoes after all.

At every moment along the way though, we need to beware. If we start trying to measure things by results, looking for 'hits' and 'highs', we are right back where we started from, playing the same old games. One of the first things we have to let go of is the idea of looking for or finding anything.

Happiness is such a strange, shifting, quiet and radiant state that the moment we declare we have found something in it, got a sighting on what precisely it is, the only thing we can be sure of is that we haven't. We may have crept close, but like a shy deer, happiness has slipped our crass attentions. So let go of 'results' too. They might be a record of an experience, but they are not the experience itself.

Keep the deer in view by keeping yourself out of sight.

How, you ask though, does one learn to 'keep oneself out of sight'? Lesson one, please, in the arcane art of 'letting go'!

There are as many ways of beginning the process as there are people. Each of us has to find our own way, all the way. More obvious starts, since we are essentially trying to unravel the mystery of ourselves, might include taking up analysis or psychotherapy of some kind on an individual basis, or joining one of the many different varieties of groups available today in which we can explore possibilities for personal growth whilst sharing the task with others working likewise. We might find a spiritual teacher or meditation instructor. We might do no more to begin with than unburden ourselves fully to a friend we cherish, or to the parish priest, or the personnel officer at work, or, if we are in a desperate state, and excruciatingly lonely, to anonymous samaritans at the end of a telephone.

In other words we are looking for someone to help us; a guide. We do not seem to be having much luck finding happiness by ourselves.

Now all this probably sounds a barefaced contradiction of what you have just heard, about happiness being something we have to find for ourselves, with foundations built on 'doing nothing' and 'letting go'. Here we are now, being advised in many cases to find someone to help us, to get involved in the complicated business of working with them so we can *be* helped. Just the opposite!

Yes there is paradox here, but since all life is an endless paradox, with the extremes of black and white being in far less evidence usually than situations composed of the two, we should not be surprised unduly.

Finding happiness in the midst of misfortune sounds a sizable paradox too, but not only is it possible, it is the only happiness able to merit its title, as one hopes we have begun to see now.

Of course, every day of our lives, our being human as distinct from a clod of earth or a cucumber ensures we have to act in some way or other, we do 'do' things, and because of that we get involved in an amazing network of actions and relationships that might seem a far cry from this hazy idea of being 'untangled', of 'letting go'. This is a realization – our 'activity that makes the world go round' in human terms – we have to keep coming back to every time we start thinking airy-fairily about shrugging our problems off. There may, as we have seen, be one or two among us disposed to acts of renunciation, 'letting go', such as joining a monastery or going off to live as a hermit in the woods, but the majority of us are still hoping to find our happiness whilst we go about our business in the ordinary world. And that's our brief here.

It is good too to get to the point where we concede we do need help in our quest for happiness and proceed to do something about it. It's good that we can confide our vulnerability and pain. We are a little more humble and open to others, less cocky, when we're forced to ask for help. As we have noted, the first step in trying to be happy is to concede openly that one is most certainly not. To confess inadequacy, seek help, is in itself to reach out to others.

At this stage, it is true, we are reaching out with the expectation of something in return – assistance – so this is not that high order of concern for others which is complete in itself and wants nothing back. That is love of a degree we do not see too often, the supernal kind. Nevertheless our own enterprise is an act of going towards others with oneself exposed to some extent, a wanting to share oneself with others, which in itself is a form of love, and a very good point of departure on this our quest.

At this point also the simple truth is that we will not know how to 'let go'. We shall be far too uptight and confused – unhappy – to be able to do anything of the kind. That is why we have had to run to others for help. We have tied ourselves in knots that have become so tight that there is no way we are going to be able to do Houdini acts and slip them of our own accord. Others have to start untying us first. They have to give us a bit of room to work in so that eventually we can begin to untie ourselves. And while this is happening, while we are confiding in others and looking to them for help, the fact is most of us are going to get pretty dependent and 'unfree' for a time in the process. In our helplessness, our needing a confessor-figure or guide, it might indeed seem that we are getting more tangled than ever.

But we cannot run before we can walk. All we can do at this stage is bear in mind that while we are looking, now, for assistance from others, there will come a time when we shall have to learn how to look for help only from oneself. Right now we must concede our inability to find any kind of stillness inside, our inability to do other than cling to things.

Yet while we cannot for the moment accomplish these higher objectives, we can still go on doing the preparatory work of trying to observe the way we behave and discover a few of the reasons why we do so in this way or that, and we can try and let a little space or detachment come between our dislike of people and things and the people or things themselves. We can try to be a little more patient and kind towards people everywhere.

We can also try not to clench our teeth in doing any of this, but make sure we enjoy the sunset framed in a window on a wintry evening's walk from work, or the plash of rain on the roof, or perhaps the soft, plaintive note from the street busker's flute . . . and we can maybe smile and even laugh at the pathetic sum of our own little woes in a world so steeped in sorrows.

It may be though that we don't want a counsellor or 'teacher'. We want to be happier, of course we do, and we are prepared to look into the possibility of changing a few things in our lives; but no, we would rather not get into that guru or group-therapy nonsense, thank you.

That's fine. It might conceivably be a pity, because good guides and groups can provide us with very clear reflections of ourselves sometimes, enabling us to start seeing the sort of people we really are and why we act the way we do, and the effects our personalities have on others, so that we can save ourselves a lot of hard work, self-delusion and continuing unhappiness. Good guides and groups, too, will not in the end let you get so dependent on them that you do feel more tangled, less free: good guidance eventually throws you out on your ear!

However, we may simply feel we are not the type to benefit from such liaisons or we might genuinely be self-aware enough already not to need them anyway, so if we do not, at all, fancy confessionals and the company of 'lost souls', there is no wisdom on earth that should compel us to do so. In this case we will make do with the raw materials to hand – broadly speaking the lives we are leading now.

Some of us may have the strength of character, the will and above all the vision to be able to carry out what in our eyes needs to be done, or undone, to make our lives more happy. Many more of us, however, having declined the idea of mentors or exposing our innermost selves in groups, will be unaware of precisely what it is we do and do not need to improve the quality of our lives, so our bid for such improvement will be a matter of trial and error, and probably no end of it, too.

Yet . . . the possibilities for change remain endless. And *any* change we attempt is valuable if we keep our wits about us, since even if it turns out to be a useless one in the end we shall at least come to appreciate the fact; learn something valuable *en route*. Fear of change is very largely composed of the fear of what will happen to us if we fail in the attempt, a terror of regret, and as a result we tend to get paralyzed by our inability to make a decision. And there is no unhappiness more severe than being stuck on the point of a pin, too petrified to move.

If, however, we can understand that any change, no matter what the outcome, can be beneficial to us if we are determined to let it teach us something, we are much more likely then to be able to plunge into it without undue fuss. If we know we cannot lose, how can we?

All this might smack of a little too much effort still in this odyssey of making our lives 'effortless'. A lot of us in this overcrowded, over-noisy world who do relish the thought of having to compete and struggle less, of having more peace and simplicity, want to find ways of living in the thick of things where they can nevertheless enjoy such advantages, and the idea of 'un-trying' and 'letting go' does not seem peculiar or paradoxical to them at all; the opposite, in fact – a straightforward matter of common sense, a good way to live.

So if they do not want the superficial razzmatazz of typical modern life, nor anything to do with therapy and growth groups, and are not exactly bewitched either by the cavalcade of fads that pass us by these days, exhaustingly, with their offers of greater wellbeing, how and where do these people begin to get a glimmer of this refreshing quietude, this uncomplication, that sounds so alluring? How can one begin to have everything one needs when one has nothing? Where can we find this inner space into which our setbacks and pains might dissolve, so that all that is left us, finally, is peace and a smile?

How can I be sane, please, in an insane world?

Chapter 4
Stillness

I used to know a woman who lived in a rather large polythene bag on some open green ground in the city. She had no family, no friends we would dignify by the name, no roof, no job, no money, no future. She was a human being apparently stripped of everything, Shakespeare's 'poor, bare, forked animal' stumbling between a hostile earth and hostile sky. Yet. . . .

Yet she kept herself clean, did not drink brass-cleaner or meths, cooked good simple food on an open fire, and gladly shared both with any other dossers to hand. She was intelligent and chatty, and enjoyed a laugh. She had no ill word for anyone or anything, though possessed a shrewd eye and brooked no nonsense. She was one of the happiest people I have ever known.

I asked her once how she stayed so benevolently disposed towards life when obviously it had heaped so much misfortune on her. She said she wasn't 'really unfortunate'; why did I think so? 'I watch the sun come up in the morning,' she announced, 'and see the seasons change. I observe the flowers and the birds and the stars and the rain. I try to do what I can to help others that want help, during the day. At night I watch the sun go down and I climb in me bag. I live: what more does life owe me? Isn't that the most marvellous thing of all – life itself? So don't you go trooping out your pity on me, young man.' You couldn't help but leave the old lady with a lump in your throat.

Now *there* was happiness for you!

No, we do not all have to plunge into exciting new careers as derelicts and tramps to find it. Most of us would crack up, probably, long before we sank that far. And ninety-nine per cent of down-and-outs are broken, wretched people. But here was one woman who was able to point straight to the heart of the matter – to the extraordinary absence of clutter around the happiness that knows itself. Happiness not a matter of 'having', but 'seeing'. Nor of 'becoming', but 'being'.

It is very difficult for most of us to see like this. In our
chasing and grabbing and hoarding, our lives have become far
too complicated for us to be able to conceive the idea of sitting
still, wanting nothing and having nothing and being able
to feel we are in seventh heaven on the proceeds. Today we call
an absence-of-things-to-do, 'boredom'. It is a boredom too that
often turns quickly to neurosis, then despair.

We are wound up like clockwork. We fear that if we wind
down we will cease to function. And so we race on.

We live in a world of Mad Hatters.

To start to come close to that appreciation of what
constitutes contentment as exhibited by the bag lady, to start
opening up that space inside ourselves which can withstand
assault, to learn how we can 'un-try' and 'let go' and 'do
nothing at all' – and yet *fly* – it is useful now, actively, to clear
away some of the 'action'; to do nothing constructively. We
have to demolish our fear of boredom.

Whether we are working now with a guide or a group, have
already initiated changes in our lives like job-swaps or taking
up new spare-time interests, and are either in the thick of
relationships or feeling rather lonely on our own, if we are
serious about pushing ahead the time is ripe for us to start
making some skilful use of our time on our own.

If our days are full we should try and clear ourselves an hour
or two every day to be somewhere quiet by ourselves. If we
have too much time on our hands, if we haven't enough
company as it is, we need to start taking a more positive look
at what we do with this loneliness. Either way we are going to
have a go at enjoying being by ourselves. If we cannot manage
this as a matter of course, we are never going to be happy.

Alone we come into the world and alone we go out of it.
Alone we are for much of the time in between. If we would be
happy, we have to learn to enjoy the fact.

The age being what it is, the moment we are on our own
these days we still have a tendency to race on; literally, a lot of
the time, if we observe the passion for jogging and running,
skiing, surfing and a myriad other solo sports. Now all these
are delightful pastimes and exercise, and they may contribute
something to the sum of human happiness. No carping at them.

But one is struck by their common denominator, a perfect advertisement for the times, which is what they offer – 'loud' sensation and speed. In all of them the world goes by in a blur. Ourselves, we get in a bit of a blur as well, a nice one; a 'high'. And the tendency is that we are denied the ultimate important appointment in the journey to happiness; the meeting, in reflective quietude, with ourselves. In a way we are running away from ourselves.

Someone might point out here that *the* most popular individual sport of the lot these days is a decidedly slow, unwinding affair altogether, namely angling. This is a pastime obviously used by a lot of people to get away from the rush and bother of modern life, in which the fishing itself is often secondary in importance to the peace and quiet it affords. Yet – there remains the excitement of the chase, all the clobber one musters on riverbank, lakeside or shore in search of 'simplicity'; all the companion anglers along the way or back in the clubhouse. We still find it hard to do nothing and be quite alone.

It might be a good idea now for us to sit in a chair for half an hour looking out of the window, simply watching the world go by but not making any inward comments or judgments upon it. Perhaps we could start to do this two or three times a week. Or we could go for quiet walks on our own more. Even if we are stuck in the middle of the city we can still amble round the park or common, the leafier streets, or up and down the old canal. And then we should try to stop thinking about anything at all, just observe the shapes of the trees, the patterns of the clouds in the sky, the colours in the shattered petrol slicks on the sad brown water. Just breathe well, and watch, and flop.

If we find it impossible to clear our heads of thoughts, of the rat-babble that seems to gnaw away at our brains all our waking hours and, we note, gets in the way of our observing things as they are, it might be a good idea – another example of our using negative things to positive ends – if we took stock of our lives from scratch and tried to add to our self-understanding.

We could list all the things we do not like about ourselves, then all the things we do. We could dwell a while on the advantages we enjoy in life, however small: a roof over our heads, food, reasonable health, the capacity still to feel and find things to celebrate over, the warm shoes on our feet, a woodwork class we get a lot out of every Friday night; a brother or sister we cherish and who cares for us a great deal. We can all make up a list if we try. We have a go at thinking positively, that's all, no matter that we might be hurting dreadfully over something inside.

This rat-babble does get exhausting, however, as one can tell at a glance from the frowns on the faces streaming by us in the street. People scurrying all over the place and seeing, responding to, nothing. People – you and I – locked up in the squeaking treadmills of our brains, even when we plonk down for some rest in a chair or take to the open heath for a breath of fresh air. How *can* we silence ourselves, for godsake?

For centuries the act of meditation, of sitting in silent contemplation, has been used by mankind as a way of cutting through the confusion in his brain and coming to rest in the heart. Once it was the preserve largely of mystics seeking union with their so-called gods. These past twenty years however, meditation has flourished more as an aid to health and happiness, and, alas, a good deal of horseshit.

If we can clean it up of the latter, however, there is little doubt that it can lay just claim to the former – and a good deal more.

The efficacy of meditation as an instrument for putting us in touch with higher states of consciousness has been well attested to throughout history, not least by our beloved scientists of the present day. There is no serious dispute left: it is a practice that gives rise to creative alpha waves in the brain, proves more restful than sleep even, aids circulation and digestion, cuts down stress and generally promotes efficiency and wellbeing. A handy tool indeed for coping with the twentieth century.

Meditation has other charms. Occult ones. In times past it made a name for itself not only as a bridgehead to allegedly divine states but also to otherwise altered ones which, it has been claimed, enabled people to do interesting things like levitate, walk through walls, live on one grain of rice a day and generally demonstrate powers beyond the wit and ken of the average commuter from Wimbledon or Westchester County. In an age as desensitized and desperate as this one for 'kicks' it has not been surprising that meditation has attracted its share of sensationalists and loons.

To see meditation, however, either as a prescription for instant happiness, or a would-be circus act, is to misunderstand its deeper purpose and, frankly, to abuse its use. It is typical that today we should seek to make something either utilitarian, or utterly fantastic, of it. 'I want to be rich and happy' or 'I want to be entertained; have my mind blown.' Between these two extremes lies the real secret or purpose of the operation. Meditation is a key to our understanding ourselves and our world. Something, in a very simple way, rather sacred.

Most of us these days understand we are (at least) two people. There is our everyday conscious self, struggling to survive and make sense of everything, and there's our deeper – if you like, spiritual – self which, we are told (and intuition and self-awareness will underline), is the 'real' us, the one in which conflicts are resolved and peace reigns, and it is this taunting, shadowy creature we spend our lives attempting to find and fuse with. The closer we come to our true natures obviously the happier and more fertile we shall be. And what meditation does, more than all the improved sex-life and business efficiency it might promote or the spoons it might bend, is slowly show us who we really are and of what reality consists.

It starts opening up that space inside us which allows us to do two things; to occupy the centres of ourselves, so we come to know much more clearly what are our real needs as distinct from our manufactured ones, and at the same time to have a 'cushion' against things that go wrong. Meditation helps bring our outer selves closer to the inner so we stop feeling so split, and relieved of the tension of this ancient conflict we are able to cope much better with our daily lives as they unfold. Very much a case of two bonuses for the price of one.

A good way to imagine the space, the clarity which meditation is able to open up in us is to think first of a jar of muddy water being shaken about. The bilge tossing hither and thither is like the state of most of our minds these days; so turbulent it is impossible to see anything clearly. Then we stop shaking the jar and let the water settle. After a while the sediment making the water mucky begins to float to the bottom. In time the water will become clear with a layer of particles and organisms arrayed along the bottom. This purity enables us now to see each little item that not so long ago joined with every other to make a turbid blur. If we like, we can examine and list the things that added up to all that confusion. And this is what meditation, unhooking us for a while from the mad merry-go-round of our days and slowing us down, helps us to do. It lets the dust settle. This then allows us to do something about it.

It is unfortunate that meditation has so often been associated with wild-eyed fakirs, pop stars, hippies and a general way of life somewhat removed from that of the majority of us – 'It's not the sort of thing ordinary folk get mixed up with', et cetera. Meditators have frequently contributed to this misfortune themselves, hinting at something expressly magical or arcane about the practice and investing it with the usual jargon of coterie or clan until it is about as accessible to you and me as ancient Greek or nuclear physics.

The truth is we are all fully acquainted with what meditation is, already. So it seems are most animals. Meditation is simply that whole-hearted absorption in something either so fascinating or so foul that we forget all sense of self and 'become' the task in hand, or the event we are witnessing.

'Lost' in artistic creation or a beautiful landscape, in laying new tiles in the bathroom or the act of making love, or even in having a ding-dong row with somebody to clear the air, we inhabit that present moment which is the only place from which an enhanced life force can emerge. Instead of myself as subject over here and the task in hand or thing perceived as object over there, I and the job and whatever tools and materials I am using in the process, or myself and what I'm observing, blend into one. Things flow, there are no more jagged edges. And when we have finished, we are alive with the glow that comes from having experienced complete harmony with something; from the fulfilment, even in dealing with adversity, of a job well done.

Even having had our row and got what we wanted to say off our chests, we feel better!

This is fundamentally what meditation is. Being who you are, where you are. No gap between the two.

To learn how to live in the present better as our real selves and feel more free of both the past and the future, to be able to silence the rat-babble and still the muddy water that pollute our sensibilities, and to have more strength to cope with setback and more compassion to extend to others, it might be a good idea, if we are of 'average' stability, not prone to psychosis (when complications might rise), to develop this practice of meditation. Without the hooha.

To be able to sit a while in silence, letting ourselves untangle, we do not have to be under the tutelage of wizards nor have studied esoteric texts. We do not need to be sitting in fancy positions with our toes touching our ears. The intoning of magical words need not entertain us, nor the fact that the nearest we have been to places like the Mystic East is the curry take-away on the corner. All we need, to be able to meditate and see if we cannot come by a little more peace and happiness, is ourselves and a reasonably open mind.

If we bring these two things to the task, which isn't really one at all, it can be virtually guaranteed that the exercise of sitting meditation will begin to make you feel better inside. If you can add to it a little light-heartedness mixed with a dash of healthy realism, the latter to ensure we do not get carried away or imagine things, so much the better. Starting as we intend to finish, remember, we should try to mix enjoyment and awareness from this point on. After all, could not meditation be no less fun, or a fad, than jogging or skate-boards?

Quite.

Sitting meditation can be done anywhere, any way you like. Park yourself in a chair or squat on the floor, or dangle your legs over a wall. Whatever is convenient and most comfortable for you. If you have a bad back you can even lie down, though there is always the temptation here for meditation to lapse into sleep. Wherever you choose, the important thing is to feel at ease. The next most important thing is to make sure your back is as straight as possible. This helps you to breathe properly.

Ensure that your neck is straight too, chin very slightly dropped; hands either in your lap, single or together, and cupped, or resting palms-down on your knees. If you have chosen the floor, a firm cushion or a couple of folded blankets tucked under your bottom will help overall posture. A blanket round your shoulders might help keep you warm and snug.

Legs crossed as painlessly as you can get them . . . uncrossed if
you have chosen a chair.

In the early days perhaps, keep your eyes closed. At all times,
no tight clothing. If you are wearing a belt, undo it.

Further aids: a quiet room or corner outside where you are
not likely to be disturbed for a while, and out of direct sunlight.
If you are indoors, a lighted candle in a dish either on the floor
or on a low table/stand in front of you will add to a peaceful
atmosphere. At the start you could stare into the flame for a
few minutes, merely observing the colours, trying to refrain
from mental acts like reminding yourself you'll need another
box of candles at the weekend or using the flame to trigger a
succession of images ranging from the lights on the Christmas
tree to the Great Fire of London. Simply *observe*.

Aha! – easier said than done, right?

This, alas, is where we start to see the sheer power of that
rat-babble. The mind is a law unto itself, utterly, like a dog
which has torn its leash and wants to race all over the shop,
with a sniff-sniff here and a sniff-sniff there. We grab hold of it
for a moment or two, hold it still, and then – wrench! – it's off
again, doing what the devil it wants. This generally is how our
minds work whether we like it or not; crazily, out of control;
which helps explain the general state of things in the world
these days.

If we are going to be happy we have to learn how to make
the mind a little more answerable than that to itself, rather than
to whatever outside itself snags its attention or takes its fancy.
However, at the onset here, do not be down-hearted.
Recognizing the waywardness of the mind, appreciating the
kind of problems it gets us into and how therefore *it*, not 'fate',
conspires against our happiness, is our first vital insight. How
do we know what we might not make of our lives if we were to
have a little more control of them?

Right now, take a few deep breaths then gently close your
eyes and settle down for twenty, thirty minutes of an
introduction to another world – your own.

For a few minutes do no more than watch (feel) your breath
coming in and out. Such a simple action, slender thread, on
which so much depends! Light, relaxed concentration on the
breath can be helped by counting it silently: breathe in, breathe

out, count One. Breathe in again (slowly, without strain), breathe out, count Two. And so on up to ten, then start at nought again. If your mind wanders before you get to ten, go back to nought anyhow.

A lot of people will find it quite difficult to reach double figures before they have forgotten what number they are supposed to be counting up to then! If you do keep failing to reach ten, don't get in a tiswas – enjoy a rueful laugh at yourself. After all, you are learning quite a lot about yourself. For a start you need a reconditioned brain!

If you can get to ten without much trouble, keep counting beyond that. But each time you discover you have lost track, that your mind has wandered, go back to the beginning again.

You can make quite a nice game of the whole business every time you meditate, seeing what is the highest number you can get to in each session.

Remember though it does not matter in the least how far you can go. You are not taking part in some cut-throat competition with yourself! You're supposed to be enjoying yourself. Nor does being able to count a hundred breaths mean you are a nicer or happier human being as a result. It may mean nothing other than the fact that you are pretty good at concentrating.

After a few sessions, perhaps three or four weeks' worth at one a day or every two days, if you have been able to keep track of your breathing quite well, reaching a consistency of counts, you can try something else.

Once you have got yourself relaxed, your breathing natural, picture in your mind a distant sun in the sky. Keep watching it, quietly. Then imagine yourself slowly drifting towards the sun and the sun slowly drifting towards you. Closer and closer. Eyes shut all the time, but make sure you don't screw them tight. Just enjoy things.

Have good, warm feelings about this our sun. It is, let's not forget, the source of all life on this planet: without it we would not be here. Through it, in the life we have as individuals, no matter how many difficulties we might be facing, we still have a lot to be thankful for. See if you can't let a few ounces of gladness rise up from somewhere. Silently give thanks to the sun.

Next, the visualized sun is so close we can feel its heat. It is a beautiful, shimmering, golden colour. There is nothing terrifying or overwhelming about this heat. It is a benign radiance such as we get from a sun-lamp. Gently it relaxes the fuddle in our minds and the tension in our bodies. We start to forget what is in our minds in fact, even forget our bodies perhaps. There is just this wonderful looming sun. It occupies all of our attention.

Then we have lost sight of the edges of the sun, it has towered over us so hugely that we have melted into it, and it into us. We are the sun now. We are the heat and the shimmering gold, there is no separation. All this we can feel. Our heart is warmth. We feel remarkably good.

We sit there, gold and empty. And we stay like that for as long as we can. When we have finished we lift up our palms as if offering something. We feel we are offering *ourselves* to others.

That's the scenario as it unwinds, ideally. In the non-ideal world though, i.e. what will happen with you and me, is that our novel form of sun-worship will not come to anything like the rather delightful undertaking it sounds above. The mind which is a law unto itself is not used to this sort of subtle, graduated control. It will soon be bored at having to sit still on a cushion and play with a stupid mental picture of a sun. Oh God, so *bored*.

So while we are camped there trying to slow ourselves down and come to rest in a state of 'nothingness', one which let's face it is going to be foreign to the majority of us, the mind will continue to fly off on the opposite tack completely; in a more frenetic fashion than ever, most likely, speeding up and desperately trying to fill this gaping hole of boredom with whatever it can lay its hands on. Indeed the mind might almost get to a stage of panic. It cannot *cope* with peace and quiet!

Off we'll go then, thinking about our less-than-idyllic sex lives, the money we owe, the holiday we would fancy in Greece if only we could afford it, the neighbour we'd like to bawl out because of his noisy stereo, the leaking roof and the mutinous state of our haemorrhoids. Something – anything – so we can keep ourselves entertained. So we do not have to face ourselves, naked.

For the same reason, we go alone into an empty room and turn on the TV or radio; so the emptiness, the silence, is filled.

Our meditation then will become a contest between keeping our minds in one piece or letting them snap into fragments that go shooting all over the place. A struggle between silence and noise.

One cannot over-emphasize the continuing importance, however, of our not making it a contest, a struggle. If we try damned hard to stop ourselves thinking, we will only get tense and sucked into a conflict of opposites ensuring we only end up thinking the more. We end up defeating ourselves and feeling sore about the whole enterprise. Back we must go and remind ourselves that we are in the business of 'not trying', of letting things go; remind ourselves of the need in all this to be gentle and patient with ourselves. Our efforts at holding ourselves still in mock sunlight are thwarted constantly by all this wild activity in our minds . . . OK, so be it!

The fact is, the human brain, those bewildering multitudes of cells pulsing with electricity, flashing and sparking like a gigantic computer, is by definition activity. Short of death there is no way we can stop it being 'active'. However, there is negative and there is positive activity, there is a machine out of control and exploding in flames and smoke, and there is the machine ticking over with the fine tuning of a Rolls Royce engine. It is going to take *us* time to 'tune' ourselves.

What we have to do right now is merely try to observe the thoughts as they keep floating across our minds. Probably, we will not observe the thoughts at all in fact, we shall be prey to them altogether and have to keep jerking ourselves out of them and remind ourselves of the task to hand – sinking into that golden sun. To and fro we will go between thoughts and no-thoughts. All quite normal, all quite good.

Our whole half-hour might turn out to be nothing more than a whirling confetti of thoughts, a set of cricked knees, a pain in the shoulder and a strong terminating desire to go out and get drunk. It might. But even if the exercise does turn out to be less of a transport of delight than a penance, do not underrate what may have occurred during it.

In the majority of cases, as I have said, you *will* feel some benefit. There will be a little more lightness, calm, inside. A little less tension around the stomach. More energy. And things could have occurred in the subconscious, beyond your immediate appreciation, that might be the start of a new adventure in your life.

There are many different ways of meditating. Some are highly complex and ideally require major changes in lifestyle if we are to undertake them properly. These are not our concern. The meditation outlined above is very simple and can be practised by anyone who can find a little time to be on his or her own somewhere. You do not need to feel, at all, that you have to have a special meditation teacher, a secret word or phrase to chant (a 'mantra'), or pay out a fairly sizable sum of money to be able to convince yourself you are getting 'value' for your effort. You can start meditating right now and in half an hour's time feel something new has happened to you.

Meditation is not about secrets and mystery, or a wonderful world of peace and insight in the future. It is a way of being very ordinary, but feeling a little special, here and now.

At its best, say when you have learned after a few weeks how to sit still in space and light for a little stretch at a time, the odd thought maybe flitting across in front of you and you smiling because you do see it as a thought, a small interruption, but do not get particularly upset by the fact any longer, the feeling one is able to experience can be something very special indeed.

It can amount to quite a gasp, the realization you have glimpsed an absolutely perfect peace and happiness; a sense, yes, of entering a new dimension of experience altogether. You have seen what life is capable of being. You have seen its fundamental emptiness, the fact you do not *have* to struggle! Life, goodness, 'God' – this, *olé*, is IT! This wonderful stillness!

On the other hand you might have found meditation an enduring chore and backache. 'To hell with it!' That's perfectly all right. Lose no sleep over the fact. A lot of meditators get so hyped up on the exercise, becoming as dependent on it for their moments of glory as does the alcoholic on his liquor or the drug addict on his 'fix', that it would have been better for them if they had not gone into it in the first place. And the bag lady with whom we began this chapter and with whom we shall end it had never sat and

dreamt up suns in her head in her life.
She made do with the 'real' one.

Chapter 5
Into oneself, and out to others

Is it not a fact that so many of our moments of happiness come when we are conspicuously not doing anything special? Sitting on a beach watching the waves break, going to bed early with a good book, making a first-class job of glueing together a broken plate, taking our partner's hand in our own as we set off down the road together . . . really, we don't need much at all to pick ourselves up; realize that life is worth living after all. The best things in life are free, we are told, but in an age where the good times have come to be so firmly associated with artifacts and exotic activities, how many of us can sustain ourselves on that knowledge even when, as we see, the wisdom of it presents itself to us over and over again?

Oh, a lot of us are given to sighing these days and saying how nice it would be to drop out of the rat race and live 'the simple life', but since the art of 'thinking simple' has become such a complicated business for most of us, of what, ideally, does our 'simple life' consist?

It consists of a highly expensive cottage which will mortgage us up to the hilt and give us no end of a headache, a fancy estate car (expensive four-wheel drive model to negotiate the rutted track leading to our splendid isolation), a massive deep freeze (considerable intervals between shopping expeditions and somewhere to store the arrays of home-grown produce we look forward to cultivating), electric saw for the exciting wood-gathering operations, back-up generator for the times when the fragile electricity supply fails, and altogether a mighty conglomeration of equipment and clothing so we can slip comfortably into the . . . 'simple life'.

Even as we try to free our lives of clutter we accumulate things. A cheap existence becomes a demandingly expensive one.

Conversely, to be happy today does not mean we have to sit

meditating all day long or going for long dreamy walks all the time in the woods, making do with one change of underwear a week and living heroically off brown rice. Even that kind of simplicity, while apparently more genuine than the cheque-book variety, can so easily possess a contrived, self-conscious quality, with preconceived notions of what will and will not lead to our happiness, which is why the prognostications of all saviours, sages and books such as this one should be regarded as so much flapdoodle themselves until such time as they have proven in your own life that they are rather more. The sort of simplicity, however, that (so this author maintains) might be said to be genuinely free of clutter is that which does not have to gnaw over the question of whether it is or it isn't.

It is so uncluttered with trying-to-become-simple it gets on with living the everyday as though it is the simplest thing in the world. In other words, a life is simple or it isn't. If it isn't, trying to make it simple is only going to complicate matters, since 'trying' is the antithesis of the non-effort at the heart of simplicity. All one can hope to do is wait for a time when it will become simple of its own accord. That is, the natural life can only come naturally. Things ripen in their own good time.

Now that might sound the perfect cue for us to shrug and forget all this self-improvement farrago; go on doggedly living the bad old life that has brought us so much unhappiness up to now. If all this trying (and un-trying) to make ourselves happier means we simply complicate things more, make ourselves more unhappy, why, again, for godsake *bother*?

Bull's-eye. One repeats: one should not 'bother'.

In the Prologue I wrote, 'This then is a book about happiness and how to find it – or rather, how to let it find you.' We cannot *will* happiness; cannot go out, grab it by the throat and squeeze the precious secrets out of it. We can't find it looking in the corner, beneath that stone or on top of that cupboard. Nor, if I do accept it is only to be discovered within myself, can I cut myself open and produce the coveted prize. Nor can I hope to get anywhere muttering, tight-lipped, 'I'm going to meditate and find it that way.' I cannot give away all my money and possessions tomorrow and expect to be sublimely happy the day after. Happiness will not jump to our attention when we crack the whip like that.

We can will an ersatz happiness, certainly. We might go out and drink our way into one, or throw ourselves into a gymnastically erotic round of sex. We could put on our sneakers and do that ten-mile run which will get us feeling *very* good. Two or three hours at a movie might do the same. But as we know only too well, these sorts of 'highs' are invariably followed by 'lows'. They are nothing to do with the happiness that lies beyond ups-and-downs.

To let happiness find us, come to us naturally, we have to do nothing other than be natural. We do not have to 'try' to do that; ironically what nearly all of us do is spend our lives trying to be thoroughly unnatural – 'faking it' so we can get on at work, be popular with the 'in' crowd, keep a relationship tottering along because we are afraid to end it and be left on our own . . . and, throughout, longing deep inside to be our real selves so we can relax and not have to perform like the organ grinder's monkey all the time. Living like this we are defensive, walled in; tight inside. Literally, we are 'screwed up'.

There is absolutely no room inside us for happiness.

This can only come to us when we are relaxed, when we are loose inside. We need, more than anything, that space inside ourselves, a big one, to allow our assorted misfortunes enough room to evaporate like wisps of cloud and assorted fortunes enough room to grow. In order to 'bloom' we have to open like a flower.

Let's see how flowers do that.

They cannot of course be commanded to do so, nor would our taking hold of the buds and opening the petals one by one by hand amount to ripeness in the least. It is true we can force the flower to open quickly by sticking it in front of a fire, but it will then merely wither and die with equal rapidity. No, all we can do to add to the speed and strength of the plant's growth is ensure it is given sufficiently favourable conditions for same. After that, the plant is on its own.

Ourselves, we shall start to open like a flower automatically when we gradually open the fist in which right now we grasp our lives so tightly.

Getting rid of the fears, uncertainties, dislikes and the like which stunt our growth; allowing ourselves to unbend and take things as they come more, and move closer to our potential, is a process of cleaning ourselves out, a purification. We do not have to add things to our daily repertoire, in the accepted sense of 'doing things'; we have to get rid of them. We have to flush out the junk.

Just as we are happy already if only we could see directly, clearly, enough; so are we wise. To be able to see to this degree we need to discard virtually everything we have learned so far in our unhappy lives, because it is this which comprises the junk. What we are being called upon to do is allow ourselves to start again. If we would enter the 'Kingdom of Heaven', which rather than being a tourist attraction of the future we might simply conceive as a state of mind in the present, we have been counselled to be 'as little children', and it is the spontaneity and unclouded vision of a child we need to rediscover in ourselves if we are to be spared the sort of sophisticated misery mistakenly going by the name of maturity in the eyes of sophisticated misers. Most of us are still sufficiently able to get glimpses of this heightened sensibility from time to time, even when we are sorely afflicted, to know that it lives on within us.

In addition to the small doses of meditation, the extra moments spent quietly on one's own and the loose-limbed exercises in general kindness and patience, together with the cool self-examinations to which we ought to be submitting ourselves all the time now, this process of purification can be aided a lot at the start by casting around in one's life, taking stock of the relationships we have in which there is strain of some kind, and pondering what might be the best way to ease them; 'clean out the dirt'. Here is an area where a little 'activity' might not come amiss.

Most of us will know someone whom we are not getting along with particularly well, where there are unspoken resentments, hurts that have not healed yet. Leaving aside for the moment our relationships with spouses and lovers which we shall look at in detail later, it's likely there will be a friend/acquaintance or two, someone at work or a neighbour; maybe a parent or grown-up son or daughter – *someone* – we have had words with or let down or been let down by, and generally come to feel somewhat uneasy with for some reason or another. And these small areas of discord can amount to fairly large obstacles to our developing the equanimity we need if we are to be happy. It is a good idea to try to dissolve them before they harden too much.

Where we have been at fault in a relationship (and guilt, which has a habit of lying around our psyches like miasma, will provide a reliable index), it would pay us to acknowledge the fact openly to the one we have faulted. It is not always easy to humble oneself sufficiently to say an earnest 'sorry' to someone, particularly if we do not know them intimately, but mustering the courage to do so can often resolve the difficulty on the spot. Sincere apologies do have a habit of melting even the hardest heart.

If they do not, and we continue to be opposed, we can try again at a later date when circumstances might be more favourable, or when time has been allowed to run its normal healing course. If we fail again, perhaps we can do no more, but at least we have made the effort and, one hopes, purged ourselves of ill-feeling in the process. The thing now, our efforts having come to nothing, is to beware that ill-feeling does not return and become even worse. We have tried and failed, and once more – so be it! We should let go of the aggravation, refuse to respond to it.

It is also important, however, not to feel quietly superior here about one's magnanimity and equanimity. Otherwise we merely cancel them out.

Apart from the tendering of apologies and regrets it is usually valuable to try and discuss with the other person whatever it is that has come between you. One should not attempt to bulldoze the other into the kind of soulful exchange one might expect in an encounter group more than in the usual run of conversation, since excessive openness will most likely overwhelm the untutored, rather than win friends and influence people. The ideal to aim for is to be quiet with one's approach, but warm and unstuffy with it.

Let the other person see you do care about rebuilding bridges between you. Touches of humour, ideally at one's own expense, are also helpful. If as is quite likely you feel nervous making the approach, don't try and hide the fact under a florid heartiness. You will give out conflicting signals and put the other person on their guard. Just be yourself. If you like, tell the other person you feel a bit nervous approaching them like this, but that you would like to clear things up and hope he or she will try to understand, and help.

Writing a note to someone, asking for forgiveness or gently explaining your side of things, can also do a lot to thaw chills in relationships. We are not very good at writing letters these days, but one that is sincerely and affectionately attempted will often prove a welcome surprise for the receiver. It is also sometimes easier for us to say in a letter what we would like to say, rather than immediately face the other person in the flesh. So look upon pen and paper as potentially useful tools in the creating of your happiness.

However, nothing can take the place of the personal touch. So do not hide behind correspondence. Go out eventually and meet your adversary face to face. And let him or her realize you are not their adversary at all.

If a split is largely the fault of the other party, the task of reparation is both easier and more difficult. Forgiving or asking for forgiveness, which is the more ticklish? It depends on the individual, though for most of us neither will come all that easily, probably. But since we are the one more sinned against than sinning here, we do on paper have an advantage in the task of clearing the air. We can shrug and let the other person realize right away that we have taken no lasting offence, that so far as we are concerned, there is no schism. From this end, end of problem.

Nevertheless we have to bear in mind that guilt and all kinds of unresolved conflicts in the other party might make them less than receptive to our approaches, still. Indeed our openness and goodwill might trigger even more hostility in them. Our magnanimity can be sick-making! Once again we may well fail, at least in the short term, in our efforts to live more amenably with others.

Failure we have to accept every inch of the way. We are not supermen. Nor are others. We are all deeply flawed and beneath the masks and armour we wear in public, all rather frail. Our happiness, we have to keep on reminding ourselves, has to flower in unremittingly stony ground.

In trying to make our peace with those we have rubbed against, or indeed with respect to whatever we do in our lives to try and improve them, we could perhaps keep in mind an old phrase, simple yet full of wise advice; a quiet plea to God (or merely a rallying call to oneself in His absence) to give us the courage to change those things we can change, together with the patience to accept those we cannot.

Viewed like that, even 'failure' can leave one with a not unpleasant feeling, indeed one of very genuine accomplishment. A skilful case again of using negative things to positive ends, of turning so-called failure into real success.

If we can keep this up we can start to realize the singular importance of what we are doing and tap the enormous energy released by the realization: simply, *we cannot lose*. Repeat it to yourself every time you run into your brick wall or fall flat on your face.

The mind that can get itself into this shape comes up with more wealth than if we were to win a fortune on the pools. Anxiety, loss . . . when, where do they ever again knock holes in our lives if we have fashioned an outlook that turns every experience into a good one?

Admittedly this kind of expertise is a long way off yet, if (we remind ourselves in our scepticism) it is possible at all. Anxiety et cetera work at the moment to our distinct disadvantage. And we still go on feeling bad about some people even though we might realize we are only hurting ourselves by doing so, or even if we have taken some truly constructive steps to try and quash the animosity between us. We cannot will our way to feeling affectionate or respectful towards people any more than we can will ourselves to be happy. We cannot be other than the people we are – agglomerations of hurts, resentments, inadequacies, fears and all the other residue of lives that have not always gone the way we have wanted.

What we can be, however, is mindful of the fact, and mindful too that others are in the same boat accordingly, and try to approach them on the basis of the humility and compassion that will arise inevitably from such mindfulness. When we have made enemies, we can acknowledge bluntly to ourselves that we have failed pretty badly in the business of relating to people, and no matter at whose door the blame might be laid, no matter that we might be feeling fed up with the other person, we can at least approach them in common humanity, put out a hand in brotherhood or sisterhood, and say, 'I'd like us to see if we can sort our problem out.'

Even though at this point we might find ourselves staring into a receding back or, worse, being laughed at to our face – if we have approached our adversary without expectation of his coming up to *our* expectations, in other words if we have gone to him with a truly open hand, so we do not get unduly upset at having to come away with an empty one, we can still gain from the occasion. We have been human, we've been brave. We cannot force others to respond according to our way of looking at things. We retreat, graciously, and so far as our re-education is concerned, move forward.

The dark corners of our relationships where we store the many unresolved problems arising from them are rarely easy places to bring light to and explore. A lot of these problems will have sunk to the farthest recesses of ourselves, hurt and bitterness burrowing deeper and deeper away from contact with that which brings them into being, and since we are effectively ruled by our unconscious, in all its shades of light and dark, we may find our lives, our relationships, impeded by things we are not in control of – time and again our best intentions will be scuppered by our worst.

Since few of us will ever have the time, money, or, perhaps more to the point, the inclination to be psychoanalyzed, and might not necessarily do any good with our lives or those of others if we were, we have to accept we will often be working in areas where we are uncertain, where there are no clear guidelines. Instead of lamenting the fact, however, or feeling that it presents us with insoluble difficulties, we should yet again turn the apparent impediment to our advantage and see to it that the lack of clarity which inevitably accompanies most relationships only ensures we approach them undogmatically, gently – accompanying the open hand, an open mind.

We have to let go the old blinkered ways in which we have related to others and viewed the relationships, that's all.

While we are shakily attempting to put to rights those associations where we do have sight of some of the difficulties – a sort of spring-cleaning in our lives, a desire to get them off on a new footing – we might find ourselves starting to let go of some friendships altogether. The inner journey towards the source of our happiness often turns out to be a withdrawal from the world to some degree at the start. This is a natural part of the process of starting to simplify our lives a little, clear away some of the clutter that bars us from ourselves.

We might find we do not need so much of the razzle-dazzle and company of old. Relationships which did not have a lot going for them anyway, which were really only very loose associations of convenience, will tend to die off naturally, painlessly. Relationships that have apparently been strong but caused lots of *angst* can start to overwhelm us. They drain us of too much energy, keep us on tenterhooks; and we may find ourselves cutting them, sometimes ruthlessly. The aggravation is not worth it any longer.

There might be many other things that begin to get on top of us now; things which contrast painfully with the peace and quiet we are beginning to explore in our walks, meditations and the extra time generally we are spending on our own – a peace and quiet which might seem strange and even a little frightening at the start but which eventually should provide refreshment, enjoyment, for a majority of us.

The hustle and bustle of modern life, its routine, the noise; the way our senses are bombarded all the time with exhortations to buy, do this, think that . . . it can all begin to get very wearying. Worse than that – pointless. However, the more horrendous the babel appears to us when it is thrown into relief by silence, the more we are drawn to the latter. The problem has a habit of procuring its own solution.

It may appear that we have yet another paradox on our hands here. If happiness is about learning how to give ourselves to others and coming to rest one day in the finer reaches of love – learning to handle situations good and bad with equal skill and not keep running away all the time into fantasies – how do we square this with our inclinations now to go into ourselves more and move away from others; away from an 'everyday' that is becoming so offensive?

The French have a phrase, *reculer pour mieux sauter*, 'to retreat in order to advance further', and it expresses a fundamental truth about the way energy works and things get done. If we cannot love others until such time as we have learned how to love ourselves, if we do not know what happiness is and are unable therefore to do very much to export it, we will only go on making a hash of things if we refuse to sort ourselves out and insist on dumping our refuse on others. Going into ourselves for a period of time is not retreating from the world if we are seriously searching for happiness, not just pulling up the drawbridge on life because we want nothing more to do with the whole sorry business, thank you.

When we approach the centres of ourselves we shall glimpse that our 'selves' as insular entities do not exist anyway, that the centre of oneself is the centre too of the whole world, and accordingly one is able to start relating to that world freely, selflessly, for the first time. Even as we journey inwards, away from others and the hurts and confusions born of our relationships with them, we shall (if we are not hopelessly embittered) find ourselves beginning to enter a world of tenderness and compassion lying at the centre, the heart, of all human beings, and therefore come to see we are moving *towards* them in ways quiet but sure, if sometimes mysterious.

It's a matter, essentially, of 'Physician, heal thyself'.

And time being the great healer – time allowed to proceed at its own pace, unmolested – it is good now to start to free ourselves from our slavish dependence on time as it has been appropriated and distorted by purveyors of ideologies everywhere, whether they are trying to sell us goods, political solutions, relationships or even – indeed – happiness. Our lives are ruled by clocks, inner as well as outer, that serve the greed and fear, the blindness, underpinning all materialism, spiritual as well as political, instead of reflecting the movements and growth of nature which end up always, if left to themselves, in the timelessness of fulfilment, of love.

Goofing off and spending the afternoon 'doing nothing' – just watching the flowers grow or the clouds roll by, and realizing how happy one can be with so little – is a political act. Tearing the oppressor's clock out of one's brain altogether, *that's* a revolution.

Chapter 6
Thinking for ourselves

To free oneself from one's oppressor and all his works – the systems that rule and generally ruin our lives, throttling us as live, spontaneous individuals – one has to learn how to think for oneself.

Many of us like to believe we do this already, but the fact is most of us are not so much free-thinkers as dustbins of other people's ideas and opinions and our psychological responses to other people's behaviour. As such we are about as conditioned and un-free as a Pavlovian dog or a Skinnerian rat. Not very exciting.

To be able to think for ourselves we have to begin the process from a mind untainted by ideas, the *tabula rasa*; a clean, an empty tablet or slate. Yes, the 'open mind'. This way we can view ideas and events for what they are and not as we like to see them. They can present themselves to us in such a way they are not instantly distorted or mangled altogether by our preconceptions and fears. Instead of judging all the time, we observe.

In according freedom to what we observe, we free ourselves.

Of course the life of any individual of mature years has been exposed to a good deal of experience, so he has come to have a view of the world of some kind, even if it is only one which says that having 'views' means we do not see it properly.

Most of us have views about good and evil; at the top and bottom ends of the scale, which is which and what we prefer. We also have common views about what is merely pleasant or unpleasant – a Tahitian beach would be a nicer place to be, say, than down a mine with the roof caved in. To some considerable extent we *are* all creatures of conditioning, subject to fairly simple mechanical laws of self-interest.

However, the worlds of imagination, conscience and love appear to operate according to more complicated, altruistic

56

ones even if, as some would have it, selflessness ultimately circles back genetically to self-interest. Whatever; these gifts, sometimes arising in inverse proportion to the boredom and suffering experienced by an individual, represent the apparent summits of human achievement, and what they have in common are qualities of anarchy or lawlessness only understood to the full, and acquired, by the . . . open mind.

Let us look at these three very special qualities and their independence of mass jurisdiction.

1 Imagination. Hemmed in by anything, whether from outside or within, it is denied its primary function, which is to explore all the extremities of human possibility and help teach us more about ourselves. This is why censorship of any kind is in the final analysis both antisocial and anti-life: evil is not defeated by pretending it does not exist, and driving it underground.

2 Conscience. This is what tempers imagination, stops me, more than any fear of judicial redress, enacting my sometimes colourful vision of machine-gunning various people I don't get on with too well. But it is something which itself has to be grounded in freedom. It has to have grown naturally within me, not been imposed as a rule-of-conduct by you or anyone or anything else. If conscience is something extraneous instead of a fundamental part of one's being, it is something we shall discard by the wayside more likely than not when it is to our advantage to do so. Ultimately one has to be free of anything, particularly incorporations such as parties and states, if one is to have a conscience.

3 Love. When we are capable of imagining the heights and depths to which human beings can rise and fall and have had sufficient experience of the worst to know its hurts, then developed a conscience which homes naturally towards the best, we are in a position to love. Love cares, not as an occasional remedial exercise or philosophical ideal, but as a way of relating to the world twenty-four hours a day. Again it cannot be commanded or regulated in any way. It does not get doled out, either, to deserving

cases only. Nor is it schmaltz: sometimes indeed it swears fairly energetically and burns down evil and corruption . . . overturns the money-lenders' tables. It is the greatest anarchic force of all.

To open a mind so that it can enjoy these kinds of freedoms, which are if you like the holy trinity of human liberty, it would be to our advantage to stop closing it down all the time with the famous rat-babble which, we begin to see more and more, is composed not so much of random psychedelic explosions (which might conceivably be quite exciting and liberating if they were) as endlessly regurgitated concepts and the worries that are their heirs; all of which are endlessly boring.

We look out on life the whole time from a kind of mental constipation.

Very early on in our lives we start developing this constipation because it pays us to do so, very much, in the sort of constipated world in which the majority of us come to live. We start cobbling together ideas (essentially other people's) in order to fit into this world – hopefully, acceptable ideas that will ingratiate us with others so that we are popular with them, make sure we do well at school, get a good job, win us influence and generally see to it that Jack does all right in life.

Apart from learning social skills which are, in truth, exercises in dissimulation for most of us, and not likely therefore to do much to enhance our happiness, we pile up huge amounts of factual knowledge about the world which, to judge by the great benefits this collectively bestows on us, appears to be about as useful as an EEC butter mountain. In a world ruled more by IQ than by natural intelligence, the more knowledge we have the more powerful we become, so it is in our interests to stockpile information no matter that it might be of no real value to anyone – even, indeed, be of harm – rather than keep an . . . open mind.

In the interest of protecting one's store of knowledge, or currency of power, people sharing common access to certain supplies of it band together and develop institutions and systems designed to exclude you and me. They will even invent a language, a jargon, to assist this process, such as the hip argot of our fashionable meditator, the Latinate pomposities of lawyers, or the psychobabble of shrinks and social workers. Government, bureaucracies, academe, the professions, all those upper-echelon industries deriving their overwhelming power from the manipulation of information and ideas, by their nature therefore attract those for whom the *tabula rasa*, the open mind, would in career/power terms be seen as the kiss of death.

And the higher one goes up the ladder the more frightened one is of course of surrendering the knowledge which has put one there. This means knowledge gets used not so much to explore the far reaches of human possibility as defend positions. As we know from witnessing on television and reading in the press what passes for public debate these days, the more powerful your everyday politician or academic, the less likely are we to encounter the kind of humility and disinterest which are the prerequisites of wise rather than expedient answers.

How rarely do we witness a true conversation, a group attempt to pool minds and arrive at a communality of experience ending in agreement, compared to the prevalence of rankling egotism and self-interest – clashes of bared fangs.

When was the last time you heard a well-known figure say, to another, something like, 'You know, I've been listening to what you've had to say and at the end of the day I have to agree you're right'? When the last time that lovely healing word of 'Sorry'?

It will be argued it is the clash of minds in opposition which sparks insights leading to more controversy and more sparks, in other words which gives rise to intellectual evolution and the growth of civilization. To a degree this makes sense, since we shall always have different perspectives about things. But at no period in mankind's history has the imperative for synthesis, in the way we relate to one another, been more urgent.

We can never be happy if the knowledge we have gathered turns out to be something we have to defend all the time. If that is the case, we live under siege. What we know is based on pride and fear – the former flourishing when this knowledge of ours brings us the glittering prizes, the latter when someone threatens to take the prizes away.

The knowledge that is more important to us, however,

which tells us how to live happily and share that good fortune with others, isn't concerned either with making a name for itself, because it knows that fame has nothing to do with happiness, or with defending itself, because it knows that if it has anything to lose, it has not found happiness.

Factual and theoretical knowledge fills us with things. But history shows us that both 'facts' and theories, no matter how powerful their sovereignty for a time, are distinctly perishable. We are filled therefore with things that not only tend to block out the light, they are also decaying in us even as they do so. Thus are the more hungry hoarders of 'things' of any kind – the rich, powerful and famous – so often made unhappy to a spectacular degree.

The knowledge that becomes wisdom, however, empties us of everything. It says there is nothing to 'know'. It does more than that really; it says nothing. This is the knowledge which does not have to 'speak' at all to make itself known, it is instead the fruit of our experience of life which does more than merely get bandied about the draughty halls of our minds, it lies in every cell of our being, it just *is*. It gets on with the living of life according to the lessons it has learned. And it knows that the first of these is that if we want to learn a lot – that is, be wise and happy – we have to be sufficiently open, all the way unto death, to allow the lessons entry to the core of ourselves, not as arbitrary rules of conduct (more 'things') but as natural, spontaneous ways of being. We do things in a certain manner not because it is the 'right' way to behave but because, for us, it is the only one.

Of course it is 'natural' for us to want to be popular, have interesting jobs that also pay for more than mere existence and, with luck, be blessed with the sort of minds able to traffic in exciting ideas. Standing outside society altogether, like the hermit, might be an effective way of throwing off a system that diminishes us as individuals, though only if we can stand aside with a smile, without bitterness. But we want to know, still – is it possible to be part of society yet not be ruled by it? Can we belong and be free at the same time?

Can we have our cake and eat it?

At one level our being free is likely to hinder our belonging quite a lot. If we do not play the games expected of us, if we show an independence of mind and spirit that is challenging (unsettling) to our masters – generally exhibit a bent for going our own way – it is probable we shall not come within a mile of the glittering prizes. So far as appearances are concerned, we might not 'belong' at all.

At another level, if we perceive that orthodoxy merely ensures we get to belong in the way a prisoner could be said to belong to his prison, that happiness can never be the home of a spirit wrenched out of true, we do not feel pain or rejection overmuch as an Outsider and begin to be aware of a very different, much deeper sense of belonging – of truths, laws, that are unchanging and a source of strength, therefore, even while societies decline and fall and take us with them.

With this 'belonging' as one's footing, conferring on one a freedom from transience and the fear accompanying it, one can walk in society with a certain spring in one's step denied, ironically, the Insider who has to worry all the time about the change, impermanence, which is always threatening to under-mine his 'belonging'. Unburdened by fear, by the task of making sure one's mask doesn't slip, the independent person can relate naturally to those people he needs to and derive enjoyment from the society they confer. The true independent knows he cannot be 'excluded' anyway: he belongs to the family of man, not just to the National Union of Closed Shops or this group or that, whether anyone likes it or not.

Then if we do not manipulate people, use them as rungs on the ladder to our own success and 'happiness', while we might find we only come to participate in fairly limited circles, the friendships we are able to enjoy in these are potentially of a quality the treadmill-rat can never know in his relationships.

They can be friendships as gifts, genuine exchanges and curiosities, not professional and social aids or emotional crutches. So in a very real way the person who is ruled utterly by society is less able to be part of it than the one who has opted for freedom. The great Insider, the famous figure who has clambered his way to the top over your dead body and mine and played the game like a master, sits finally on his summit, surveying all, in the greatest loneliness of all.

This freedom we are looking for will acquaint the honest seeker, however, with his own quota of loneliness along the way. If we are going to strip ourselves of the set ways of doing and looking at things that have thwarted our happiness, inevitably without our props we are going to feel naked and vulnerable after all this time. Important milestones in growth – the sudden, perhaps awesome discarding of things that do not assist it any longer, the trying out of new perspectives which might – can rock us to our foundations. We haven't many guides or guidelines any more. And the more determined we are to dispense with half-truths and safety nets in the quest for the whole truth, the more we are likely to find others pulling out of the journey with the odd shudder, forcing us to go on alone. Real happiness then is not for the faint-hearted!

On a more encouraging note, once the mind has been prised open a little, and a little more, the aperture can sometimes start opening thereafter at a fairly bewildering rate and introduce us to whole new worlds of being and relating. It can become a *very* exhilarating business – if, that is, we do not expect it to be, or plan it.

But first things first.

First it's good to take a look at some of the things this mind of ours does not take kindly to, over and above matters like torture, corruption and such which in readers of a tome such as this we will, if we may, take as read. What gets up our noses? The Conservative Party? The lead pollution said to be damaging the brains of our children? Bloody Arabs? Punks? Laboratory experiments on animals? The ghastly whining voice of some female 'star' on TV?

Take a look at some of these kinds of irritations. Carefully. Ask yourself what is it about them which makes you react like you do.

The lead pollution and vivisection will prompt a quick response, no doubt. About things such as injury and murder – goddammit, you *care*! It is an instinctive compassion for the victims together with a revulsion at the sort of society that permits such things, no matter what the end benefit might be to some.

That's fine. But we would do well at the outset of course to examine all the facts of the cases before subscribing our moral outrage. That way we might not waste it!

You see, right away we are encountering what we shall

continue to run into every day of our lives, the fact that there is nearly always another side to every question, a different view. And happiness is helped everywhere by ourselves developing the grace, openness and sheer common sense of accepting the fact and trying to work skilfully, accommodatingly, with it. The imposition of one person's view on another by force of one kind or another is the story of all our struggles, revolutions and wars. These will continue to be necessary on occasion, regrettably, to enable us to *resist* such impositions. But meantime, a way to work towards a time when man might stop imposing his will or ideas on others is to learn how to stop doing so oneself. We need to defeat ignorance and darkness in the world, first, by doing so in ourselves, then trying to dispense a few of the proceeds peacefully, and particularly by example.

Second, if peaceful persuasion fails and it is shown beyond reasonable doubt, for instance, that petroleum lead does poison our youngsters and is continuing to do so unchecked, and 'They' go on blithely killing millions of defenceless animals for benefits that in no way redeem the offence to our humanity, then we may have to do something practical about the matter. We can line up and halt traffic in the streets or deliveries of rabbits at laboratories, or engage in a hundred and one possibilities of disruption and protest.

What is important here is that we get to this point not because we have been swept along by a rush of emotion or by rent-a-crowd, or by being brainwashed in any way, which is the sort of thing that happened at Nuremburg and is still repeated nearly every night on our TV news from one corner of the globe to the other, but because we have come to a decision after having cleared our minds sufficiently to think for ourselves.

It is another example of how we can 'belong' and yet stay free.

As for the Tories who make our toes curl (or the Republicans in America or the 'Liberals' in Australia; whatever), the reason we have voted for the left all these years . . . while we might perceive the ethos of the right – that the human being is inherently selfish and that appealing to 'enlightened self-interest' is the most creative way of organizing him – as a gross misreading of what we yearn for in our hearts more than anything, which we declare to be community and sharing; can we not stand back a moment and acknowledge there are elements of Conservative faith, its championing of the individual against faceless governments for example, which speak extremely pertinently to us in the age of increasingly regimented societies? Do Labour's trade unions and all their works bring us one whit closer to a world that's 'excellent' and free?

In other words is the other side always wrong while I am always right; and if so, do I not engage in a tyranny of righteousness?

Adding everything up I may decide to go on voting the way I do, but would not my understanding of how the world works be enhanced if, say, I went on supporting what I believed in, the cause of the left, whilst diligently listening to the voice of the right? And tempering each with the other?

Bloody Arabs and Punks? Do I know any? No? Is not my horror of them founded on information received? Arabs, right, are rich idle sods with cruel ways and Punks are impecunious idle sods with same? If I do happen to bump into either in the street, is not my immediate resentment based on nothing more than ignorance and fear? I know next to nothing about these creatures, and their strange dress and ways threaten the stability of the way I look at the world and think people ought to behave. They are an offence to my concepts.

But in recoiling from them with the curled lip do I do anything to promote greater understanding and harmony between people, and so add to life? Of course I don't. I only make sure the Arab goes on thinking Englishmen are cold, aloof, racist snobs and that the Punk persists in his attitude that 'straights' are Death. Wonderful for everybody.

Finally, what about the woman television personality whose voice grates on one's nerves like a dentist's drill? Is it the voice itself, really, which upsets us? Or is it not perhaps the fact it is a 'common', 'non-U' accent which is offending our idea of what we prefer our broadcasters to sound like . . . or, at the other end of the scale, such a toffee-nosed drawl it raises the hackles of our egalitarian principles? All round, here is a situation where we start to dislike a person not because of who or what she is particularly, but merely because her voice, which after all she cannot do very much about, symbolizes something *I* do not care for.

As we can see from even this little list, most of us tend to be alarmingly intolerant as a natural way of relating to people and situations. But if I am going to feel bad about Arabs and Punks etc. in a world full of them all, is it likely I shall ever be able to find a place in that world, especially one become a global village in which old tribal lines are dissolving so rapidly, where I can feel at ease – find happiness?

You may skip in to argue here that surely there is no chance of our doing that anyway in a world where anyone who has not yet had a hole drilled in his head is bound to feel 'bad' about something or other – the dictators who oppress, the poverty and hunger wasting millions, the injustice and corruption everywhere, and so on *ad infinitum*. 'I feel "bad", "very bad" about these sorts of things, so how can I ever sit back and feel "good"?'

We may accept that bigots as well as out-and-out villains are 'no hope' contenders for happiness, but the wider problem remains – how can good, decent people themselves ever hope to find it, either, in the kind of society we are living in at the end of the twentieth century?

Chapter 7
Accepting

There is of course an important distinction between feeling bad about Arabs, Punks, etc. and feeling bad about people having their genitals electrified or being forced to beg in the street. It is the difference between prejudice and compassionate anger. Yet we *can* do something with both to help us grow into good citizens who are nevertheless happy in a bad, unhappy world.

Prejudice is something we can start attacking with gusto just as soon as we have mustered enough courage to recognize how badly we are contaminated with it. This is 'our' problem as individuals, not 'the world's problem', so we can get on with working with this one every minute of the day.

Resorting to our rigorous self-investigation once more we begin to mutter 'Ouch!' quietly to ourselves every time we come out with a put-down or curse on someone, something else. These tend to pour out of us without our even having to think about them, normally. They are the dregs and lees of all our concepts and fixed ideas about things. Now we *are* going to think about them; note the appalling frequency with which we criticize others and feel smug and correct about ourselves.

'Jesus Christ, what is it about women that you can never ever get a bloody straight answer out of the creatures!', 'Oh, Dickinson, he's dead from the neck up', 'Janet's always sucking up to the boss', 'One thing I hate more than anything is blue-rinse matrons baying for blood', 'He's a right 'nana!', 'I do wish one day he'd fall flat over his absurd notions and break his neck' – our days are filled with our brilliant expositions of the follies of others and our sentences upon them. But what happens if we persist with this kind of outlook is that eventually the years pile up with disillusion, scorn and finally, most likely, contempt and hate.

Each time we are wilfully negative we should try to note the fact. One could even keep an approximate daily count. By the

end of the day do not be surprised if you have found you must
have spent most of it *moaning*. A lot of us spend our whole
lives doing just that. This is not only a handicap to our being
able to find happiness, it is simply bad for one's health. It has
been noted that people who are quick to criticize others and
slow to forgive are found in abundance in the cancer statistics.

Self-correction of this kind will not come easily to most of
us. If our vocabularies are liberally stocked with sighs, groans
and words like 'disgusting', 'footling', and 'farce', what we are
asking of ourselves is the learning of a whole new way of
thinking and talking. If we are repentant, and earnest about
trying to stem our floods of misanthropy, misogyny, etc., we
may find for a while now that we have nothing to talk about or
comment upon at all. We will render ourselves deaf mutes
almost.

Others might think something peculiar has happened to us,
or that we have gone sick.

If after having spent twenty years tearing everything to
pieces and eating secretaries for breakfast we march into the
office one morning and chirp what a lovely day it is and how
sensible the government's new proposals seem to be, we are in
danger too of giving our colleagues heart attacks.

Altogether it can be a very strange experience indeed. Also
after a very short time quite an exciting one, again. Catching
ourselves out, starting to trace the patterns of our responses to
things, seeing how hopelessly we rise like fish to a fat worm all
the time instead of possessing the coolness, the space, to be able
to react both more sensibly and imaginatively, can be such an
eye-opener that we get quite hooked on the whole business.
This is good. We are not having to don hairshirts and whip
ourselves to improve ourselves: instead, this self-study lark is
quite a fascinating *game*!

In which case, enter right into the spirit of it.

If by ten o'clock of an evening you discover you have
totalled twenty-five incidents (thirty-five, fifty . . . ?) of bad-
mouthing this and sneering at that through the day, and
therefore been a distinguished curmudgeon, go take the dog for
a walk to the 'local' and have a celebration pint. Clearly, you
are not deluding yourself. In this enterprise of stripping oneself
to the marrow you are doing a fantastic job! So do not feel

down-hearted. On the contrary, treat yourself to a little quiet pride along with your beer or whisky.

(A further instance of using our errors to buck ourselves up – recycling the rubbish, etc.)

In learning to disengage ourselves from our tendencies to lash out at things and see life generally from pessimistic perspectives, we are not being asked to surrender our critical faculties. That would be daft. Unreal. It would even be counter-productive, since happiness as we know now is dependent on awareness, and awareness at the level to which we're aspiring asks that we are *very* critical indeed . . . but critical of ourselves most of all, and always criticism, wherever it might be directed, without malice and with compassion. In other words our criticism is not something we launch at others as a defence of ourselves, not a tilt in uncontrolled anger or retort. Instead, it is a tool we bring to a disinterested study of a problem that seeks a wise and thus effective answer.

If you stop and think about it a minute, in stopping ourselves being so mindlessly critical of everything all the time, we are being asked to exercise (self-)criticism of a particularly stringent kind. So, no, this learning how to be more tolerant is not asking us to turn ourselves into jellies. But it is only when we have started to learn how to be more accepting of others and situations we do not always immediately understand or sympathize with, that we can develop the tolerance, the compassion, that will allow us to respond to barbarity and injustice *with* some form of individual action.

If we have spent our lives being prejudiced, feeling 'bad' about Arabs, Punks or whatever – generally unsympathetic towards everyone and everything we do not agree with – we can hardly be expected to feel sufficient sympathy and anger to act on their behalf should *they* suddenly find themselves victims of repression or disaster.

True compassion has to be indivisible, and to be indivisible it has to be a way of life.

Otherwise we are likely to fall into that trap again of wanting to change the world out of a sense of rage/resentment, or because we want power or simply because we are so confused that we feel this is the way we will be able to find our personal happiness. Hence all the rhetoric, terrorism and revolution that get nowhere – because not enough of those involved know how or what it is, in all its myriad facets, to care.

Take away 'the enemy of the people' and shoot him and you have forfeited the right to expect other than that 'the enemy of the people', were the boot on the other foot, which it usually is most of the time, should do exactly the same to you. The rhetoric of your principles and justifications, no matter how poetic the former and apparently practical the latter, cannot excuse the *fact* that at the end of the day you have acted in precisely the same way as your opponent and therefore cancelled your assumption of moral superiority. In addition, to be realistic about it if we look at precedent, you have demolished the hope of your action ever leading to any real improvement in anything. Thus all the revolutions that finally do no more than live up to their names; literally going round and round in circles.

So we have to feel sufficiently *good* about people and our world right now as we go about our ordinary business, in order to feel sufficiently *bad* about the injustice being perpetrated everywhere to want to do something effective about it for a change. If we do not accept people enough to care about them, the more likely are we to accept the horrors that keep getting heaped upon them. Indifference is all.

But once committed to the relief of those made to suffer, it is vital to ensure that a difference is maintained between one's own outlook and behaviour and those of the people causing the suffering. It may happen we shall be forced to kill, reluctantly, in an emergency, in order to defend charity and justice, as we have conceded, but at each stage along the way, if ever we are to change the hearts and minds of men, we have to try to ensure that charity and justice wait on our general progress.

We must never lose sight of the four things necessary for all social change of any substance. First there is the supreme valuing of the individual, the insistence that he or she must never be used as a means to an end, since the individual, microcosm to the world's macrocosm and therefore inexorably connected to the larger good or evil, is himself the 'end', and the 'end' will always be aborted if that which constitutes it, flesh and principle, are aborted *en route*.

Second, this anchorage of the grand vision within the individual is secured by holding fast to those three things that will always prevent our being swept away by the words, commands and actions of the mass; imagination linked to conscience and love . . . that which guarantees my internal freedom – and yours.

In the end then, acceptance of the individual leading ultimately to love of him brings about non-acceptance of the systems and ideologies which are always trying to subject him to suffering, invariably 'for his own good'. This is our answer to those intellectuals and activists who sneer at acceptance as an exercise in mystical hogwash, a 'cop out', and a way of shoring up the status quo. It is the person who has never learned to accept anything, feeling endless anger and resentment towards those with whom he does not agree, who if he does get his way will merely vent those qualities upon those he has vanquished and himself perpetuate the status quo.

The action that is truly radical is one which does not postpone the New Dawn till tomorrow but, in the teeth of all opposition, gets on with it today.

Once more we begin to see that, just as acceptance does not mean appeasement in the least, happiness is not remotely a matter of feeling chuffed about life all the time. Life being what it is (the 'bad, unhappy world'), it would be unrealistic to expect us to react to it as a matter of course with a shrug and a smile. Because our happiness is based on caring for others, we are bound to experience suffering on their behalf even if we do manage the unlikely feat of triumphantly dissolving our own. So long as others hurt, we shall.

However, just as it is important in our quest for happiness that we learn to accept others more, so we have to learn to accept what happens to us even as we go about the business of not-accepting some of the things that do! More double-takes and paradoxes, here we come . . .

It's simple, really. Until such time as we live in a perfect world there are always going to be lots of things a sensitive person with a conscience will not accept and in many cases must actively oppose. If I care deeply for you I am not going to 'accept' someone, some regime, spiriting you away to a dungeon in the middle of the night. I am going to do all I can to get you out. I'm going to experience a lot of fear and upset while I do. I may even care sufficiently for you to be prepared to lay down my life in exchange for yours. Eventually I may for instance join with others in an armed attack on those who unjustly detain you. By now it might seem that matters such as 'happiness' must be the least of our worries!

Naturally, experiencing fear and upset, we would not conventionally be called 'happy' at this point. Yet deep down, in that universal space a person can find within as a source both of refuge and understanding if he is sufficiently, diligently gentle with himself, serenity can be tapped and used to sustain one even now. In the middle of our pain it is possible to be in touch with peace. In the middle of our flurry of action, we are able to be still.

Happiness here is not champagne and laughter, accolades or even the quiet idyll of the walk beside the stream, but the ability still to love and do what one must in its service no matter what the price; the un-caring become the caring that is all one ever needs to be happy. The acceptance of a duty of non-acceptance. The acceptance of 'doing what I have to do, and there's an end on it'.

It is the happiness of having a direction to go in even though there may be no tracks, little light and a terrible storm; and no one to guide or comfort us *en route*. All it is is the quiet sureness of knowing 'This is the way'.

Acceptance of fate, which we find when it can no longer sway us from our deeper purpose, we have to cultivate by finding the 'quiet sureness' of a direction in which to go. We have to have something to go towards; a target we do not lose sight of.

This will simply be a vision – our vision of a better world in which love, kindness and common sense prevail; our 'deeper purpose'. But it won't just be a fanciful picture of what might be, which is the way both of the textbook revolutionary and the romantic, but a flexible design-for-living we adhere to here and now.

So, each time we get kicked in the teeth not only have we to learn how to pick ourselves up and carry on, we must try to return again and again to our vision, in order that on the one hand we are sustained by it, and that on the other we sustain *it*.

We have to remember our brief. Nor must we grit those teeth, doing so. We are trying to 'purify' ourselves, remember, all the way.

And time and again we shall be kicked and cast down. Life is like that for most of us, unfortunately. Yet each time, if we're going to get to that peace-beyond-the-storm, the calm eye at the centre where we can look out and see everything that is happening to us with a degree of dispassion, we have to learn more and more to let go of the blow and our reaction to it. *Whatever* happens, we go on!

In this way grand vision and daily life learn little by little to be one. We are able not only to dust ourselves down after a setback and be strengthened in coping with daily life, at the same time we constantly soften ourselves on our vision . . . until one day, perhaps, there will be no more 'coping' to do. Instead, inside one's being, the vision is all. One becomes one's internal sun – the truly happy man.

That sun we have been dipping into in our meditations we can use also as an aid any time during the day when things start going wrong for us. If we feel overrun . . . cannot handle this or that . . . it can be quite a help if we can shut our eyes for even as little as a few seconds and plug back into our visualization and what it symbolizes. It might even be useful to give the sun a face in order to humanize it a little – a very personal, 'sun' face. Something strong yet gentle with that all-knowing, gnostic, Mona Lisa smile. Or, since we are using a lot of things in our quest as mirrors to ourselves, we could give the sun our own face, so it is there in our minds looking back at us and smiling ruefully, sighing, but ultimately pulling a face at us with a certain amount of self-parody and a serpent's hiss that we get off our backsides, stop snivelling and 'get stuck back in'.

Used like this the visualization becomes an 'indwelling spirit' or personal talisman, a reminder of the grace, goodness and sheer warmth we would like to bring into our lives, and not only can this provide us with temporary relief from the stresses and strains of the day, if used with the right gentle concentration it will prove to be a remarkable little generator of energy and grit for many of us. Try it and see. Of mere auto-suggestion and 'heart' is such magic made!

So as we cuss and froth through our days and get struck by

thunderbolts and pigeon droppings, pausing to correct ourselves whenever we realize we have behaved badly or reacted foolishly to things such as when we have hurled two fingers all over the place and made gorilla faces at people whenever they have crossed us, what we are doing in effect is embarking on a way of behaving which is a constant meditation. We do not meditate only on our cushions in the candle-light (if we do that at all); we do so if we possibly can all the time. A different kind of meditation it is true, but it leads to the same end, *the taming of our minds*. And practice round the clock, on your toes, is infinitely more valuable than half an hour a day on your bottom.

The more aware we become of what is happening in our minds so that we understand gradually why we behave the way we do and can correct our more obvious errors, the more control we will have over our lives, the less we shall feel threatened by what is happening to us, the greater will be our acceptance and love of things, and the more frequent and deep our happiness.

To be practical, a lot of us are not going to find acceptance of events any more easy than acceptance of people when we look at some of the things that do happen to us. If my wife and family are wiped out in an air crash or I discover I have less than a year to live, or your little girl is brutally raped, equanimity is going to be a difficult commodity to come by. Apart from the direct pain we suffer we are thrust back into the old problem of 'higher meaning' and the collapse most likely of our being able to make sense of whatever that might mean. How does one accept a world which is so relentlessly feckless and cruel? With things like these going on, how can there be any noble Grand Design?

If we believe in God we may have ready answers: 'His way of testing our faith, tempering our spirituality', perhaps. Or 'His judgment on our wickedness'. There is a growing theological idea, however, that maybe God is not quite in such control of things as we might care to believe; that He's 'there' all right but He *isn't* Mastermind; there are forces He does not control and His purpose is to help us come to terms with things as they are as best He can. Others who believe in God may, as we have noted, find that disaster shatters their faith: 'If there is a God and he causes things like these to happen, he's a cruel joker and I want no part of him.'

The truth is that none of us can prove to the person next to us what *is* the meaning of our lives or why such terrible things do occur in them, or what happens to us when the breath gives out; and while we might with no difficulty devote an entire and interesting lifetime to the study of such questions, as not a few people do, the further truth is that both speculation and catechism do not by themselves do very much to guarantee an improvement in the quality of your life or mine. Indeed, philosophizing about the Meaning of Life is more likely to make it meaningless for a majority of us. Only ourselves, by our own observations and actions, can find out what is its meaning for *us*.

How do we act though in a way that is 'meaningful'? No difficulty: we behave well, with kindness, even when our luck is at rock bottom. Why? Because our observations show that while the good man does not always appear to get his deserts – that kindness and civility aren't necessarily reciprocated in this world – the evil one *always* gets his due. He may enjoy wealth and power for a time, but we do not have to be Harley Street psychiatrists to glean how essentially insecure, afraid and unhappy he is. His face, words and actions say it all. And his eventual, inevitable dethroning concludes the farce. Behaving badly does not win us jot or tittle in the end. So the common sense we make rather a lot of in these pages tells us we will not find happiness doing the devil's work.

Then, whereas bad behaviour always gets its due in this life, there are sufficient instances known to most of us where kindness and its cousins *do* get paid in kind, where people who are just and gentle in the face of adversity do appear to know something about the secrets of happiness, and where sheer nobility of an individual's spirit proves it is able to do something wonderful to the hearts of a crowd. So our common sense dictates we go in this direction rather than the other.

It is this observation, so simple yet so profound, that good (understanding) does have a small, measurable advantage over evil (ignorance), which is what ensures that men and women continue to come together, that children are born, that homes and workshops are built, that flowers are planted and music is made; all in all, that we go on 'going on'. It is the triumph of hope over adversity, an important element in the story of our evolution.

It has been said that in the struggle between good and evil so far, the former must always have had at least fifty-one per cent of the share of the human psyche, the world's spiritual energy, and that the moment it slips to forty-nine and evil takes control, that is the time to cut and run to the shelters, brothers.

So I do not know why I am made to suffer and weep and get up every morning to live another day. I have a few theories, but they are not and aren't ever likely to be anything much more than that. All I do *know* is that I am here and it makes sense on the evidence before me to try to live this life as happily (constructively) as I can. I do know that when I am mindless and harsh on others, as I am too often for my liking, my life comes to have no meaning and be harsh to my touch. When I reach out, sometimes I get my fingers burned, but now and again my hand gets taken into another's, and I into their heart. When in the mountain night, alone, I reach out to the stars, they answer me, they fill me with joy. Life may still be 'meaningless' so far as metaphysical explanations go, but that does not matter. What is important is that at root it *is* beautiful, and sometimes it's fun.

In the absence of a set of printed instructions at my birth it seems a good way to journey, to me. To travel lightly, accepting the life I have been given yet remaining curious about its destination, and lending a hand along the way – what more?

Chapter 8
Ending the war between head and heart

Why do so many of us grow unhappier the more we lose sight of our youth and early hopes? Surely through experience, through discrimination, we ought to learn how to be happy much more often, as a matter of course?

Why doesn't our knowledge-of-the-world help us more than it seems to? Where is our 'discrimination' falling down?

In one sense the increasing discrimination of age is extremely valuable to an individual's development. When we are young and fresh we like to taste everything we can get our hands on in order to find out what we fancy or what is good for us, and what isn't. We gorge ourselves (and frequently make ourselves sick) in the cause as it were of educational research.

So as we grow older and cultivate our tastes a little, preferring this at the expense of that and not wasting our time on things which no longer do much for us, we shape clear identities for ourselves that announce to the world who we are. At best this identity will amount in maturity to a discriminating wisdom; a sense of self-assurance.

At worst, however, and all too often, it becomes a label tied round our necks which slowly starts to tighten and choke the life out of us.

The trouble is that once we have grown up a bit, say reached the second half of our twenties or early thirties and got ourselves established in the world to some extent, it is usually much less trouble to accept the label. The world of profit and loss and technological hubris finds labels much easier to deal with than people. The group syndrome we have looked at, using knowledge as an instrument of power and status, exerts an enormously powerful influence. To survive in this world of groupthink, which is the one with which most of us are familiar, we begin even while we are relatively young to shut down the process of growth because this implies an endless

76

moving-on which we fear will lose us our convenient and profitable label, and endanger our survival. We grow to be like the robots which are taking us over more and more.

But of course we cannot stop ourselves growing. Our deeper selves are 'moving on' all the time whether we like it or not, and when the conscious self proceeds to grind to a halt because it craves 'stability', 'security' and what have you, we have a classic situation of conflict and a potentially classic recipe for psychological breakdown.

So while I may have got to an age where I am a middle manager with a handsome wife and two children, a four-bedroomed detached house in leafy Commuter Country and a caravan and a car, and prefer Scott Joplin to either Mozart or Meat Loaf, feel the country has gone to the dogs because the working class has grown bone idle and the likes of my executive superiors are clueless buffoons, believe young people today haven't an ounce of the wit and wisdom they had in my youthful heyday of the 1960s, and want the government to do this and that as a matter of urgency if society is not to fall apart, it would pay me not to cling too tenaciously to my proud vision of myself as the backbone of the nation, Suburban Man.

Deep down there could be a fire-eater, homosexual drag queen or Trappist monk screaming to get out.

Having found what we like to think of as 'us' in life, we settle for this, not wanting over-much to change our idea of self and rejecting anything that does not quietly reinforce it. We have found a reasonably comfortable niche, label, self-image and way of life, thank you, and from this point on, the years will not add very much to this except disillusion. The more disillusioned we get, the less we *accept* anything. We just come to feel tired and angry and altogether fed up. We get stuck.

So most of us as we grow older do not grow wiser at all. We shrivel. When this unfortunate process is well advanced, we shall rail against the whole world; become cantankerous, unconsolable, wasted old souls.

What we should be doing as we grow older is not narrowing down in the least but the opposite – growing. Growing out, not 'in'. Becoming wiser, accepting more and more instead of less and less.

This does not mean we throw overboard our fancies for this

or our very intense feelings about the grotesquerie of that. I shall, if I may, continue to opt for wine in favour of whisky. Salads instead of steaks. Also I will go on contesting discourtesy or, more serious, people who treat other people like dirt. The architects and officials responsible for a good part of our urban development and the human misery it has engendered over recent years I would sack, subject to inquiry and parade for a modicum of public accountability through the streets. And so on.

What becoming a little more skilful in the art of living does mean is that if neither wine nor salads are available I shall not fret, that discourtesy will be met with confrontation which is courteous, and that the victims of one's scorn will not find it attended by one's hate. Once more, one learns to live with things even as one goes about either refusing or opposing them. It is difficult to foresee a world which would be free of all of the things one does not care for, so waiting upon their removal for one's happiness would most likely be a protracted business.

If we do let ourselves narrow down into mere attitude and prejudice as a response to life, we deny ourselves the possibility of encountering the new experiences that might keep our days sufficiently varied and interesting to make us *want to go on* experiencing more of the same, and give us that chance to grow. It is only by accepting this possibility and what it brings with it that we are going to flow and not end up in that constipation which to all intents and purposes brings life to a standstill.

Our difficulty is that we bring to our examination of the problem and possible ways of solving it the sort of constipated thinking which has got us into the mess in the first place. It is like pouring oil on fire. Not very clever.

The only way we are going to make a sizable inroad into the problem of how we think and behave in new ways is to do so from the outset – we are back to the business of the destination being the journey and starting as we seek to finish.

Lying awake at night grappling with a difficulty in our minds . . . we are probably all familiar with this process and what it usually bequeaths us: a headache, awful tiredness in the morning and rarely very much of a resolution. We should not be surprised. If it is our deeper selves which harbour the quiet voices telling us who we are and what we should be doing with our lives, we are hardly likely to be able to pick up these signals through the babel of our divided conscious minds.

With the latter all we do, endlessly, is go this way, then check ourselves and go the other way, then check ourselves again and return to the first path, and traipse back and forth and back and forth until our brains start to crackle like badly tuned radios.

Since our conscious minds, reflecting the duality expressed everywhere in the phenomenal world, see everything as a struggle of opposites, sometimes admittedly a lopsided one with a particular set of ideas having very much the better of another lot, but nevertheless always engaged to some extent in going round in circles, we need to cut this vicious circle with the voice of the subconscious which has been digesting the fruits of our arguments from the day we were born, feeding them to the 'real self' for scrutiny and coming back with the 'real self's' answer – *what is right for us*.

To be blunt, we have to shut ourselves up in order to hear ourselves speak.

The deliberate attempts we have been making to slow down and simplify our lives a little have all been directed to this end. Taking time to be on our own, attempting to look at things with our brains 'disengaged' for once, meditating and the rest all help us develop a better feeling-tone in our lives so we are not left to the mercy all the time of a mind that can never make up its mind! We have been trying to give ourselves the room to let intuition come and speak its mind instead.

As we know from the testimonies of distinguished figures, scientists and artists alike, many of their far-reaching discoveries and finest works are not the product of tying themselves in knots and banging their heads on the wall. The opposite, indeed. It has been in reverie, trance, daydream, sleep dream – generally, the unguarded moment – when inspiration has struck and the Muse has spoken; when the individual was able to get in touch direct with the resolution to the conundrum that stalled or with the reality that moved him.

Archimedes it was, dreamily soaking in his tub, perhaps playing with a toy duck while he found what he was looking for, who gave us not only one of the most joyful exclamations in history but a supreme lesson in living, the fact that things we seek tend to come to us readily enough when we have learned how to relax and let go a bit.

In our deliberations about ways and means of becoming more happy it may be that we have thought about divorcing our partners or changing our jobs; doing something pretty dramatic with our lives at any rate to try and change them for the better. Big decisions like these may go round and round our internal debating chambers for weeks, months and even years. Usually, it is safe to say that if we have been this bothered by the idea we ought to go ahead and do it. The grinding mills of our minds have a habit of spending ages chewing the obvious into mincemeat. We could spare ourselves much energy and headache, however, if we could learn how to contact our inner voice early on so we can be helped to come without too much agony to 'clean' decisions which work for us.

If we do no more than look coldly and rationally on our dilemma, add up the pros for ending our marriage and then the cons, all we are going to end up with is a catalogue of items, dead as a shopping list, which takes very little account of the fact that any relationship other than one perhaps between two computers or cold-hearted schemers is founded more than anything on feeling. If we are to find out whether it would be better to end this liaison, we need to get in touch with this, urgently. If we have little or no skill at doing so, we are faced with a Problem.

Left to make up our minds purely on the basis of 'reason', we may make a decision that violates our unconscious needs and, ironically, propels us ever nearer the time when we so lose touch with this deeper self that we start behaving thoroughly *unreasonably*.

If we are at sixes and sevens with ourselves we are going to be at sixes and sevens with everything.

A lot of you, however, may still feel uneasy about letting the irrational side of you have its day. We have been brought up to equate irrationality with mumbo-jumbo and disorder, and it is of course curious and telling that an age which has striven so hard to rid itself of the irrational should find itself so awash with . . . mumbo-jumbo (propaganda, groupspeak, journalese, etc.) and disorder. It is not, however, surprising.

If we cultivate reason to the exclusion of the irrational, we can hardly hope either to be knowledgeable about the latter or skilful in handling it, with the result that its intrinsic waywardness is always going to go on undermining the neatness and order of our revered intellectual enlightenment and making a mockery of it, which in a nutshell is the story of this century in particular.

So our task of unbending our minds even as our bodies bend with age, of shedding some of our dogmatism and rigidity in the way we look at the world and giving ourselves the opportunity to let other ways speak to us, is not only an important element in our quest for happiness as individuals but a vital one for the security of the whole world – which, we do not have to be geniuses to appreciate, amounts in the end to the same task, even if it is one that is never likely to be finished.

If you are a worshipper at the shrine of reason (and until such time as the mystery of life is sorted out, this approach to the problem is as much an article of faith as any other), believing firmly that only the will, the act, can solve problems anywhere, cast your mind back a moment to those occasions when you have struggled to remember someone's name or a piece of valuable information that has suddenly slipped your mind. What do we do?

We try to remember by concentrating hard. We *force* the brain to give up the mislaid information. Then if it stubbornly refuses to do so, as invariably it does, it is likely we shall start getting mad at it and cussing ourselves out – 'My God you're turning into a senile old duffer' sort of thing.

Here is a perfect illustration of so much stress (in all senses of the word) being put on reason that we end up behaving quite irrationally. But of course, if we will push the swing too hard in one direction, elementary laws ensure it must then swing too hard in the other.

We lose the space at the centre of things where the rational and the irrational meet in mutual assistance, and act as one.

Now, having got fed up with trying to remember our 'lost' name or whatever, we go off in a huff. We give up. It's pointless, we cannot for the life of us recall what we are after. Then what happens?

After a while, which might be only a matter of minutes or as much as a few days, we are walking along the street or sitting at home browsing through the paper, thinking about nothing in particular, when suddenly ('Eureka!') the name or the information which has eluded us pops into our heads like something coming home to roost. No fuss, no pack-drill; it's 'there'.

The information we seek about the way we should run our lives so we can feel more fulfilled and happy, what decisions we should make and things we should do, and what we should not, will often come to us in this manner if only we will let it.

For the most part, true, it will not flash across the front of your brain in big capitals like an electronic billboard – YES, YOU SHOULD END YOUR MARRIAGE PRONTO or NO, FOR GODSAKE DO NOT STAY IN LONDON. Nor is it likely to come to you as a literal piece of action in a dream: Muggins packing his bags, leaving a tearful spouse at the door and marching triumphantly into a honeysuckled cottage with a ravishing new blonde on his arm. But 'what you have to do' can come to you with no less certainty, even so.

This certainty will be that prized feeling-tone inside you. The 'true self' is speaking to you not in the way someone might sum up the pros and cons of a debate and finally pass judgment on the argument, but as a quiet, gentle sureness percolating through your whole being. You do not need to debate. You *know*. After that, acting is no problem.

I do not pretend for a moment that the faculty of being able to hear the quiet voice within or exercising the courage to act upon its advice will be something we discover overnight. Yet many of us are already in touch with that source, only we are so in thrall to the whims and fancies of others at the same time that we are afraid to be who we are.

How many times do we know instinctively what is right for us – 'I would do this if only I didn't have to think about that' – but turn away from what needs to be done in favour of what 'has' to be ... because we are afraid of social censure or a future maybe denied a few of the comforts that have accrued like barnacles to what for the most part discomfits us, or a less than wholesome past that might catch up with us unless we are careful? How many times do we heed the advice of others, usually preaching accommodation, at best a caution, instead of listening to what we hear in ourselves?

We need to be careful here.

Spontaneity, which is a way of looking at the world and acting based on the kind of inner freedom we have been exploring in these pages, is the great prize we are after, but it has nothing to do with what is popularly meant by the word. If by spontaneous we mean doing the first thing that comes into our heads, there and then, and our heads are not screwed on properly, our alleged freedom from constraint is not likely to do very much for anybody. In fact one way or another it's likely to be downright harmful.

This kind of 'spontaneity' is impulse, not insight. An essentially selfish act, not a wise one. When asked afterwards why he behaved in such a way, the impulsive person will say, 'I don't know, I just did.' The one behaving 'naturally', that is who is being true to himself, and skilful, might also say, 'I just did', but the difference here is that he will know why he did so. He acted in that way because it was the obvious thing to do, an advantage to everyone in the circumstances prevailing.

Our being 'free', 'flexible', 'open', 'instinctive', 'spontaneous' and all the other appetizing things you keep hearing about in this text is not a matter therefore of refusing to deliberate on issues and taking the easy way out – of suddenly turning on your heels and walking out of your marriage, for instance, because your husband is getting on your nerves and your ego is getting a much better deal from the loose fish who is massaging it and other delectable parts of you on the quiet.

Here you have a marriage beset with real problems and all you are doing basically is running away from them and a self whose selfishness and lack of understanding generally happen to be major contributions to those 'real problems'. So 'spontaneity' here, running after quick gratification and away from our pain, means we only drag our problem with us, to be sure it will snag or engulf us again before long.

Here is a case where irrational behaviour is getting us into all sorts of trouble; where the administration of a little reason itself would be useful as a stiff corrective.

If instead we had listened to our subconscious it would undoubtedly have told us that our behaviour was singularly stupid. Because we have not listened, because our inner voice has not been in touch with the outer, reason itself is impaired.

We neither act 'reasonably' nor in a way that is in accord with what we truly want. All we could be said to be doing, really, is flounder in the dark, a state of mind occupied by not a few of us these days.

So you see, learning how to open up and accept things, to drop concepts and be spontaneous, is not in the least a matter of cheerfully throwing the brain out of the window. Since the early 1960s there have been many advocating death of the intellect as the gateway to reality and happiness. Drugs, sex, touch-therapies, dream yogas, stream-of-consciousness literature and art, the cults of karmaic and astrological predestination, loud music, magic, burning down cities and all kinds of 'mind blowing' recipes – these have been inevitable, and not surprisingly given rise to many excesses and absurdities, in an age which has yearned so painfully to know how to feel again after two centuries of scientific rationalism which has dried up the springs of our joy, our wisdom, and turned us into spiritual and emotional eunuchs. Withering on the vine our lives, our hearts, have cried out for refreshment. We have longed to be inspired, to be able to wake up in the morning feeling the day ahead offers fresh adventure. We have become weary of the insanity perpetrated in the name of reason. Yet genuine spontaneity, the exercise of wisdom, insists we have to be wary too of the insanity perpetrated in the name of its opposite. Each dearly needs the other as a mirror and check to itself it we are to be both intelligent and sensitive, and whole and sane, and thereby free.

But learning how to let go and get back in touch with our feelings is what most of us need to do after the long sovereignty of intellectual pride. Usually we are still lopsided in favour of too much head at the expense of heart.

Happiness itself is merely the moment when the two conclude their ancient conflict, each seeing there is no longer anything to fight over, nothing to win; when, as with Timon of Athens, 'My long sickness of health and living now begins to mend, and nothing brings me all things.'

Chapter 9
Tasks like unemployment, or being alone

Yet, the reality remains: when we are confronted with 'nothing' in our lives, when the bottom suddenly drops out of our world or all our plans finally crumble over a period of time, we do not find anything very funny or rewarding in the fact. Disaster *floors* us.

Even if I can turn my gaze heavenwards and derive some consolation in my misfortune from the fact I believe there is an Incumbent up there, I tend nevertheless to go on being unhappy.

All right, we have had a little abstract theory so far about coping psychologically with being kicked in the teeth, developing the mental attitude which will help us. We have looked at a few ways, generally, of doing so. Yes, in theory at least, you are maybe with me so far. But the fact of the matter is that all this advice and encouragement has gone nowhere really when confronted with reality. This of course is what commonly happens to theory. So perhaps we ought to take another look at the problem, dealing with specifics from a ruthlessly practical angle.

Let us take a situation, a misfortune, which is all too common right now; a person say whose marriage broke up last year and who has subsequently lost her job, this year – insecurity about relationships and employment being two of the banes of the times (for us fortunates not of the third World where more basic incapacitations and terrors prevail).

The woman in question is no longer as young as she used to be, is living alone on the dole and feeling increasingly depressed. She has done the usual things to try to help herself, such as consult her doctor (and perhaps, unwisely, submit to Valium or such) and avail herself of the support of her friends. She has tried to keep reasonably active and not skulk all day under the bedclothes, groaning. Above all she has tried hard to get another job. And she has also had a go at shaping her mind along some of the lines we have looked at in this book. All round, the lady is no slouch, no fool. But behind the activity and awareness, endlessly there lurks despair.

What more can she do? Or 'not do'?

The apparent twin pillars of her unhappiness, the fact she has neither partner nor job, need to be looked at carefully again. OK, the lady interrupts, I know my problem here is that I am suffering from 'unfulfilled expectations', 'too much wanting' and all of it, but I can't help it. What 'I know' cannot cope with how I feel!. So how do I cope with the fact?

I think what the lady needs to do at this point is not struggle to 'pull herself together' in the least. The stiff-upper-lip approach to coping with misfortune is more concerned with putting a face on it than understanding and doing something constructive about it. We are made to feel guilty if we give way to our depression. We are even threatened with penalties if we do so – harm to our social and professional standing. All that repression does of course is make us feel more afraid, depressed, than ever.

So perhaps it would be wiser to indulge the depression a little. This means going into it, letting it take you over for a while. By not getting tangled up in resistance to it, which as I hope we understand now will only make things worse, we allow ourselves to explore this depression, find out why it is hanging around as long as it is and maybe see if we cannot find a gentle way to slough it off.

Depression is an illness. Sometimes it can be fatal. Therefore if we are sensible and compassionate we ought to treat the patient tenderly, kindly. We do not fight the poor brute! Instead we see the unhappiness we feel right now as being downright healthy of us in the sort of world in which we are living, something also shared by a few million other customers even as we languish here in our own stew. I stop struggling to be 'happy in the moment'. I can't be. Full stop.

Looked at with a certain insouciance, unhappiness after all is nothing very special, so why do I make such a song and dance about it? *That's life*! (The kind we have created, anyway. . . .)

Next, the matters of having no one and no job. Assuming that you did have a partner and some work to go to, would these in themselves guarantee you would be any happier? We know from experience that they would not, indeed we know that some partners and an awful lot of jobs could be guaranteed only to make us even more miserable than we are right now.

The position is then that we are likely to be unhappy whether we have a partner and a job or not. With an 'ideal' partner and an 'ideal' job we think we would be happy, but experience again tells us that the ideal in life appears on the scene with rather less frequency than the ordinary or the makeshift, so if we are ever going to surface from these doldrums it would be intelligent of us to recognize that the practical solution involves neither partners nor jobs, ideal or otherwise. The solution involves one thing only. Ourselves.

Once we fully appreciate this we can perhaps start to break that exhausting round of feeling unhappy when we are in a relationship and unhappy when we are not; bored when we have a job, bored when we haven't.

No one can be truly happy in a relationship anyway if he or she cannot manage without one. No one can be truly happy in a job if he or she can't manage without one. This is because in both cases our happiness is dependent on things outside ourselves, things which can and most likely will be swept away in the remorseless sweep of time, and our underlying fear of this happening will always nibble away like woodworm at whatever contentment we might like to think we have fashioned, meantime.

As soon as we can see then that clinging to others, to jobs or to anything at all will always deny us the great ease at the centre of genuine happiness, we can start to do something about the fact. I am alone, I have no job: *here* beginneth and endeth the lesson.

Let's take our solitariness first. If we spend the whole time hankering after 'Mr Right', weaving fantasies around the gorgeous creature, we can hardly be said to be involved in that process of giving ourselves body and soul to the moment which is the only activity which can put the sparkle into it.

Half of us is stuck here in our woe, half dangling over there in Wonderland, and we are therefore no more 'complete' than if we had been cut in two by a guillotine.

Any happiness from this situation is only going to come when we take the base metal of its singular ordinariness and like alchemists transmute *this* into gold. As a gnomic Jewish saying puts it, beautifully, 'The only whole heart is the one that has been broken.'

The fact is I'm a forty-four-year-old divorcee with greying hair living on under £50 a week (1992 prices) in the company of half a dozen wilting plants and a moth-eaten cat, and this, *all this*, contains everything and all the happiness I can ever know. Leaving my four walls and hurling myself into feminist politics or sexual abandon, studying under Jesus Christ, putting my savings into a face-lift, bicycling to Samarkand to give myself 'space' to think . . . all these things and more may help me in one way or another, but eventually they must all propel me back to the place where the gold is found, in myself within my own four walls.

This being so, we might decide to take a short cut, or fast road, and live dangerously. If my room is the world, there is essentially no escape from it. If I do not learn how to live there fruitfully I shall soon come to feel I am locked in a cell. If I do find a way, the room being the world shall cease to have walls, fears; and after that I shall be free. Anywhere.

'The way' is dangerous because it is so simple. When human beings who have spent all their lives on a treadmill have it taken away from them, invariably they go to pieces. As we know, perhaps the greatest human fear of all is freedom. Be brave, however, find it, and that is the end in this life of all our searching. We can live at last in peace.

Perhaps the prospect of the solitary room is not such a terrifying one after all.

Living there 'well', alone, we let ourselves see if we cannot enjoy our own company. We do not plan ahead making sure we have somewhere to go, something to do, every night of the week. We do not hang around willing the telephone to ring with 'hellos' and invitations. Nor do we slump around the place gawping at telly the whole time and getting sloshed on Home Brew. Every attempt to turn away from ourselves we check with our self-searching. I am here, the only guest, and I shall see to it that he or she is treated accordingly.

In our daily round there is a skilful balance to be found

between routine and leaving things to chance. It is wise to make sure we eat simply and nourishingly, with as much variety though as possible, and enjoy the perhaps strange ritual of dining alone. Try not to eat with one's nose in a book or the box on, distracting you from yourself and your food and the magical union of the two! Also, look after yourself in matters of cleanliness and grooming. Wear attractive, comfortable clothes. Your home itself – make it more than 'a box for living in' no matter how ordinary the place might be; an expression of yourself if you can . . . clean, reasonably ordered and with a splash of flowers. Don't pretend otherwise: even on the dole we can afford a few blooms.

Be wary though of trying to escape into obsessive care of the place. That only betrays the fact you see the external world as a hostile realm, Chaos, and are struggling (rather pointlessly) to impose order on it. Don't have a routine for looking after the place, just a sensitivity to what needs to be done when it does.

What you do to fill in the long hours of your unemployment will depend of course on your personality, interests and so on, and while it will be good to continue spending some time doing nothing, simply relaxing and 'observing', you will still want to find something to do (apart from job-hunting) during the acres of free time left you.

Creative pursuits of all kinds, getting out into the community doing voluntary work part-time, reading the books or undertaking the projects you have always wanted to tackle but never had the time for while you were a 'damned wage slave'(!), perhaps getting to know your neighbours a little better if they are also around during the day, using the cheap or even free council baths, gyms and sports centres in your neighbourhood to lick yourself into physical shape, sitting down and looking seriously at the possibility of a major career change anyway – opportunities for the unwaged themselves to enjoy constructive and interesting days, taking a further step in the direction of your happiness, are thick on the ground if you are determined to look them out and use them.

Which brings us to the *problem* of our having no work anyway. Clearly unemployment is one of the major sources, if not the major one, of our unhappiness and insecurity as a society these days. Brought up on capitalism's Protestant work ethic by which an individual comes to define, to value him/herself only by his or her job, the loss of it naturally results for that person in a loss of self-definition, self-esteem. The correlation in the industrialized world between unemployment and ill health, higher death rates (including murder and suicide) and increased admissions to prisons and mental hospitals is beginning to look depressing enough in itself. 'Where there's life there's hope,' it is said, but since hope appears to be diminishing sharply as forecasts point to even crueller unemployment ahead, the lives of many of us as they stand appear distinctly doomed. In theory, happiness looks increasingly like a dead duck.

As few of us nowadays appear immune to the threat of unemployment, if we are going to find a happiness that can survive it and similar disasters it looks a good idea to see if we cannot re-evaluate our attitudes to labour whether we are drawing a wage at the moment or not. Here is an area where tearing the oppressor's 'clock' out of one's brain, bringing about a revolution in our consciousness, might be considered supremely important. If we can pull it off, seeing joblessness not as the end of the world but possibly the beginning of a new one, we shall have worked ourselves into a psychological shape for the future, found a flexibility and courage – even perhaps a small sense of excitement – boding well for it. We can never be happy in the present if we go on being lumbered with foreboding about the future.

So let us see if we cannot slay the outsized dragon of 'work'.

Of course mankind wants to work or do something with himself, at least part of the time. The urge to do so comes as naturally to the majority of us as does the desire to make love or be in touch with Nature. It is an important component in the make-up of the whole person. Without the impulse to design and build – generally create – things, no doubt we would still be squishing around as primitive life-forms in the cosmic soup. But if we want to work or 'do things', we prefer to do so in a way that is satisfying and meaningful for everyone concerned. Which of course is where the problem starts.

As British trade unionists Clive Jenkins and Barrie Sherman have written of the problem today, 'By and large people neither enjoy their work, nor do they enjoy travelling to and from it.

Most jobs are repetitive, require little if any personal initiative and, for the most part, people are incapable of fulfilling anything like their full potential through them.' Spot on, Brothers.

In this situation, overall, we both want work and don't. We are cruelly divided. Not much of a formula for happiness, of course.

What makes things worse is that if we do not have work (no matter how awful, soul-destroying, etc. it might be) we feel the immediate pinch, from a financial angle, since we have been brought up to equate happiness with spending. We are also made aware of an immediate social pinch since we feel (with some justification) we are stigmatized. And we feel poorly altogether since without anything to 'do', without money, social worth and esteem, we are utterly lost.

It might pay us in another way to pause a while in our lives here and reflect on the fact that while we place so much importance on work as a means of acquiring income and social value, the proportion of our time actually spent doing that work is almost marginal. In the eighties, for example, Britons (including children and the elderly) spent only about nine per cent of all their time at work, compared say with the thirty-seven per cent they spent sleeping.

With the working week and duration of working life likely to shrink to a marked degree as advancing technology kills off more and more of the shoddier jobs, as the remaining labour cries out to be shared more equitably and as we drift more towards leisure activities under the triple influence of dire necessity, vague inclination and perhaps formal education, the impact of wage slavery could soon be even less than it is for many of us right now – in terms of hours. But unless we do something about our attitudes to work right down in the cores of our beings the impact of wage slavery, if only through our feelings of such as deprivation and panic, could grow worse.

We cannot change society's attitudes overnight. But we can make a start on changing our own here, difficult though the task will undoubtedly be in those cultures where we have been brainwashed by establishments and churches to believe that 'the devil makes use of idle hands'.

Seeing that some of the 'idlest hands' on earth might be said to be found in the great houses and churches of our masters, such a gospel is nothing if not curious, if not in its own way apt. And it is by looking into the reasons why we think the way we do about work, into the pressures on us to make sure we have jobs at any cost, that we can perhaps undermine our slavish adherence to the work ethic and ponder alternative ways of finding our happiness. We have to stop being taken for a ride.

Taking that pressure off ourselves by our own initiative reduces severely the ability of society to frighten us, and automatically therefore increases the prospects of our being able to find happiness within ourselves.

We feel guilt about not working because we have been brought up to do so. There are of course many parts of the world where what might be termed the *mañana* ethic is more in evidence, so it would be hard for us to insist that having our noses bent to desk or grindstone and working for material gain, or in order to pass the time, is innate; a disposition of all cultures. In our own the conspiracy between leaders secular and ecclesiastical over the centuries has used the work ethic to keep the working masses in their place. It persuaded them that economic salvation lay in piling up profit for society (essentially those who controlled it), and that through this activity emerged one's spiritual salvation (and, not altogether fortuitously, the economic profit too of the church . . . and essentially those who controlled it).

If we can begin to understand how we have been coerced into acceptance of something we do not always feel at ease with (who in their right mind wants to be a workaholic?), it will help us come to reject it – in this instance not of course reject work *per se*, but the tyranny that work has helped implant in our psyches. This subtle tyranny is a far more clever, profitable form of control than driving individuals into factories by force or sticking them in work-camps. So we shall spur our cause, our happiness (self-sufficiency) as individuals, by deciding that being forced to let go our grip on the work ethic does not have to be interpreted as a disaster; on the contrary, it could be seen to be no bad thing.

It is a nice irony that what is now forcing our grip off the work ethic is an economic order that initially planted it in us, which is an indication of the contradictions inherent and coming home to roost not only in capitalism but, since no other social and economic structure has yet improved on it in terms of being able to supply us with the universal happiness, found in all systems – and as observation and common sense tell us, in life everywhere, if only in that everything eventually wears out. In learning how to handle the economic changes now being forced on us we are facing nothing more than the to's and fro's of nature, of history, so it might help us put our recession into perspective if we gently remember that. We are not being faced with anything which is new.

A Nobel Prize winner, economist Wassily Leontief, has drawn a parallel between the plight of the conventional worker today, feeling threatened by the new technology, and the position of the farm-horse when the tractor arrived. And we know, particularly graphically from the novels of Hardy, about the lot of the rural worker as the Industrial Revolution began to break up the old, settled patterns of country life. The drudgery of either draught-horse or peasant is nothing we would wish to avail ourselves of today, of course, and history teaches us that a time will no doubt come when we shall look back also and shudder at the drudgery to which the mass of industrialized man has been forced to bend himself this century and last.

Things are changing, and very quickly, and maybe there is more room for celebration in some respects than for gloom. At least, perhaps, we should keep ourselves alive to the possibility in these difficult years of transition.

Our forty-four-year-old divorcee who has been made redundant should not only try to 'cope' with her joblessness, therefore, filling in idle days with physical jerks or charitable works as a way of keeping tolerably sane and thereby as it were marking time, but try to be creative in the fullest sense, using the situation to develop a fundamentally different, more pliant attitude about having spent half a lifetime being a cog in a machine anyway and seeing whether there might not be ways of developing oneself to become more than that in the future.

If she had a pastime that had rewarded her with a lot of fulfilment there would be a good case for trying to see if it could be expanded into a way of making a living, if only a partial one. 'Happy are those,' it is said, 'whose hobbies are their work.' Indeed. If she had some savings, perhaps from a small redundancy payment in this instance, it would be revitalizing, morale-boosting, to look into the possibility of her investing in getting such self-employment off the ground. If this was achieved, even if in a small way at the beginning, the energy released would prove a remarkable fillip after the lethargies and miseries of unemployment (and maybe too the lethargies and miseries of the employment preceeding it).

Linking up with others in a similar position would be another constructive way of exploring fresh career possibilities, pooling skills and resources (sheer bloody-mindedness included) and again giving rise to the spring of hope. It could be argued that instead of merely dispersing one's energies in protesting about unemployment, demanding the supply of more of the same old boring, exploitative jobs (which is where radicals sometimes come to grief, logically), it might be more liberating in every sense if our heads and hearts went into creating new jobs for ourselves that gave everyone more control over their lives and on the way enabled us to bypass 'Them', The Establishment, be it right-wing or left.

Naturally, there are many of us, the older members of our communities particularly, for whom the psychological wounds of unemployment will be especially difficult to heal, who have few immediately apparent resources of any kind to be able to pick up the threads and start again; what one writer has described as 'people with something that's died inside them, so they are like wounded animals dropping out of the pack'. For these the task of ever finding the acceptance and inner strength to know happiness is a daunting one; but not impossible.

For in the end not even old jobs or new jobs or surrogate jobs or anything society might dream up to keep us occupied so we refrain from taking to the streets and burning things down out of frustration and boredom will give us the happiness we crave, since this cannot be got from the having of anything, only from an ultimate freedom from all things enabling us to care for them because we have no need to possess them. And this freedom from things is as available to the ageing shipyard worker fallen on hard times as it is to the mystic in his cell.

He may not have much of a chance of ever finding employment again, but if the discarded worker can sit and study his hurt, see it is no more than a continuation really of the wound he has known all his adult life, inflicted by a system that never had a lot of time or compassion for him and used his work to 'use' him, but recognize gradually that the dereliction of the wharves and cranes has its echoes too in the lives of those who have exploited him; that everything thrives and moulders and moves on; and that in the midst of it all there is still the unknown of the future, the excitement of the young children on the quays with their ships' dreams and the call of another world in the cry of the seabirds, it is possible perhaps for him to see the final futility, the vanity, of all striving and come to rest even in this life bit by bit in peace.

There *is* hope. As journalist Anthony Sampson has noted, even in Britain, where there is some of the worst unemployment anywhere, there remain scores of 'half-dead' industrial towns and cities where their inhabitants are doing their best to look after one another; exchanging fruit and veg from their back gardens and allotments, bartering things and doing odd jobs among themselves. The patterns of family life and friendship still operate and compensate for social life lost at the workplace. And our long traditions of close communities with privacy built into them, of leisure and gardens, could perhaps make us better equipped to manage the process of de-industrialization than most Europeans with their competitiveness, cooped-up apartments and crowded streets – or, it could be argued perhaps, Americans, whose definitions of success are so psychologically demanding on individuals.

I have a suspicion that the UK, the first country to get into the industrial age, might be the first too to get out of it – and into the kind of world we shall need in any that follows. As Sampson has, I think, wisely, pointed out, it could be that in tomorrow's world psychic balance may look more desirable than industrial zeal; perhaps the division between the haves and have-nots might come to lie in the difference between individuals' inner resources.

These, we recall, are the only ones we can ever safely call our own.

The success of the future may lie in our being able to understand and act upon the subtle distinction between jobs and work. Jobs that pay us money we may or we may not have, and our material lives will in a majority of cases reflect the fact, but work – all of us to a greater or lesser degree can profitably give our lives to this. For those of us in the more affluent countries in particular, this will be the work of ensuring we as individuals survive psychically so that communities can survive likewise. The decline of international prosperity, energy and hope in the past few years has left few of us with lives untouched by the outcome – by the disease of despair especially – and 'work', that which needs to be done, stares us in the face in whatever direction we care to turn.

Once we can find work of this kind, a commitment-of-care to both ourselves as individuals and to others as communities of individuals (and not as abstract herds), then we are not in the least 'unemployed'.

With 'nothing', no set ways of working or looking at things, only reaching out to others whilst having a go at letting go of the rubbish in ourselves and trying to kick it out of the more encrusted, unresponsive of our institutions, can we triumph over the dole queues and the prophets of doom.

With 'nothing' and everything to do, we are likely to find ourselves extraordinarily busy.

And not unhappy while we're about it.

Chapter 10
Responsibility and the way of Quality

While post-industrial society struggles to be born, upheaval is not only going on 'out there' in the world, naturally it's going on inside all of us as individuals both as 'victims' of change and, let us not forget, also as agents of it. Unfortunately a lot of us only see ourselves as 'victims'.

We are preyed upon constantly by hostile forces outside ourselves. We have little or no personal autonomy. Basically, we are powerless.

This all too common view of mankind, passive and pessimistic, does not give people very much credit for being able to make their own choices in life. And so, pervaded with a feeling of paralysis and hostility, such a view sees violence, the overthrow of the dark forces strangling it, as the only solution to its dilemma.

The misfortune here is that such action even if successful does not do very much to resolve the problem of the dark forces within ourselves. Our unresolved private conflicts then only go and create others in public. We are back to square one.

As creatures who have been conditioned to a large extent, our lives affected by happenstances over which we appear to have had little control, we have of course been moulded by political, economic and social forces seemingly far greater than any of us. We have often been the victims of injustice and evil bestowed cynically in the official name of the greater good. It is no difficult matter to crush the dissent, the spirit, of many of us. The individual, we are fondly taught in the twentieth century in particular, cannot stand against the mass, so it is only in the mass that he has any hope of discovering his happiness.

The idea of personal responsibility falls into disuse. After all, there is something to be said for not having to think for oneself any more. It saves a lot of effort.

We close our eyes; shrug more. The smell of burnt flesh in the smoke from the chimney at that 'secret defence establishment' round the corner – we are duly surprised, very, when it is pointed out to us. We change the conversation to the price of sausages, or the weather.

Night-times, after a fashion, we'll make love.

But when individual responsibility is thus eclipsed, the word ceases also to have any corporate meaning. We drift into the all too familiar world of steamroller power, and passing the buck.

As individuals we start to feel trapped. We do not much care for this stifling, frustrating, dehumanizing mass into which we have been driven/driven ourselves in order to scratch an existence, a place; but we do not much care, either, for the diametric opposite, going off into the blue on our own and leaving the mass behind. We want to 'belong'.

When we see there is nowhere to go, that we can't be 'free' in the physical sense, usually we start getting hopelessly depressed.

Yet whether we choose to stay, toeing the line, or go, declaring we want no part of 'this sick society', both avenues illustrate our reluctance to shoulder responsibility, in the first case for ourselves and in the second for others. And it is precisely this reluctance which makes us unhappy. Cowering abjectly in society, being overrun by its demands and precepts, having little or no say in the running of our own lives, we have little hope of being anything other than miserable. But running away from society, hating it and all its works, still leaves us with division inside, so once more we condemn ourselves to anything but peace.

We start to see now that the search for personal happiness and for the social good cannot be separate enterprises, and that the only way we can come closer to either goal is to assume a personal responsibility for both. With this responsibility we can ensure that personal happiness and social good act as a system of checks and balances for each other. One will not do anything for oneself that would harm the greater good, nor freely do anything in the name of the greater good which would harm the individual, oneself.

By deciding to take responsibility for our own lives, our actions – in effect to grow up – we are able to overcome the handicaps of heredity, upbringing, bad luck and all the other things we are wont to blame for the fact we are afraid to stand alone and test to the full, having 'nothing', what it is to be human as distinct from a cipher.

By taking responsibility upon ourselves in the present we are able to free ourselves from the past. And we open up the possibility then of a future that can be fundamentally different from that. Such, generally, appears the best hope of any effective social change.

Responsibility of this kind will enable us to fashion an individual life of genuine choices even while we belong to the mass. It allows us to see what we must do when society behaves unjustly: as we have noted in our discussion on conscience, we must oppose, even perhaps at painful cost to ourselves. Responsibility also allows us though to see what we must do to ensure society tries to behave well: it impels us to propose. And it does not allow us to behave badly towards other individuals for the sake of advantage to ourselves.

So we have a good practical code to live by, here. It does not matter that society's might on the whole be different – that in this cynical age a lot of people might think us a 'sucker'. That is only an opinion. By this stage we might be coming to the point where opinions as such, whether one's own or those of others, do not carry so much weight as they used to. Opinions, after all, are to life as droppings are to food.

'Responsibility' has had a particularly hard time of it lately, though sometimes the way afflictions are being handled in the industrial communities today does appear to illustrate some revival of interest in our mutual obligations as human beings. But, at large, the cultivation of personal freedom which half the world has seen as the way to fulfilment and happiness has been brutalized time and again into something else, the cult of supreme selfishness . . . the road to supreme unhappiness. This aberration has been brought about to a considerable extent by the abandoning of . . . responsibility.

For it was this, itself, which was widely interpreted as a singular impediment to our self-realization; it had connotations of repression, of codes of conduct designed principally to serve the interests of the Establishment. These codes stank of piety, hypocrisy and manipulation. Ruthlessly, we began to root them out of our lives. We even enjoyed a few carnival years of gross irresponsibility as we tore up the past: we entered the age of 'doing your own thing', and for a while it seemed jolly. Then darkness fell.

The long history of 'responsibility' as a tool of class interest and social control followed by a brief explosive one where we nevertheless failed to recognize its importance as a *guardian* of those freedoms we sought for ourselves – frankly, we ought to have been wise enough to see this coming. It was only history's 'boomerang effect', whereby one excess or duplicity sees to it that it is followed by a counter-excess/duplicity. By the same token, for instance, we could have foreseen that the much-trumpeted Sexual Revolution was destined to lead to the cult of celibacy said to be chic at the moment.

What however is needed now as a relief from repression on the one hand and anarchy on the other is an individual and social freedom-with-responsibility, but not the kind commonly preached by politicians, who at the last nearly always equate responsibility with the interests either of class or state.

Since the interests of either class or state have always served finally to set one man against another, the responsibility that seeks to bring men together must be rooted in the eternal wisdom that knows how to do this, and since neither class nor state can itself be wise until the majority of its members are thus, the kind of freedom we are talking about can only be vested in the care of the individual.

In the end the only refuge of *Liberté, Égalité, Fraternité* and the truths that encompass them is the human heart. So our responsibility as individuals, as guardians of the good of the commonweal, is considerable.

Responsibility means therefore that we as individuals *won't* shrug in the popular sense of the word these days and be party to the indifference, rudeness, wilful obstruction, lies, cheating and the general full-time occupation of taking short cuts at every available opportunity which have become the flagrantly accelerating characteristics of our official dealings with one another and add up to such an indictment of our claim to be social beings. Here is another instance where 'acceptance' in the popular sense is not our idea of the word at all. This cynical acceptance of the growing wasteland of our days does nothing either for our development as individuals or that of a more just, humane world.

If as an individual *you* rip people off, fiddle your income tax and pass the buck all the time 'because everyone else does', you have no right whatsoever to gripe about 'the state of the world'. No right to expect other than that others will short-change you. No right to happiness at all.

Many radicals argue that society has rotted beyond the point now where qualities such as justice and humanitarianism have any hope of winning the day in what remains. Society as we know it has to be destroyed. Anything that helps that process is to be encouraged. To wit, steal and cheat the system, debase the language which itself has been used as a tool of repression, stir up as much hatred and resentment as possible in people, render the neighbourhoods where they live more intolerable so all they feel like doing is destroying them; dress and behave in such a way as to illustrate the madness and futility of everything. Such are the politics of despair.

On the other side of the fence, the argument of many traditionalists likewise is that our society has rotted beyond the point now where there is any 'hope'. Society as we knew it *has been* destroyed. The most we can do, those of us with anything left, is to hang on grimly 'for the remainder' to what we do have and augment it bit by bit when we can. To wit, steal from the have-nots and use the system to keep them in their place, debase the language so words like 'freedom' and 'responsibility' can be trotted out glibly to buttress our interests, leave the poor to founder in their hatreds, resentments and intolerable environments, dress and behave in such a way as to illustrate that we do not give a fig about what is happening beyond our privileged redoubts – such, again, are the politics of despair.

But as neither of these (familiar) attitudes to life offers hope of remedial change this side of the Collapse of Everything, or exercises any of the kind of responsibility which can set us free from the tyrannies of either, our search for happiness must logically drive between them and pass beyond.

Since life does go on for the moment despite everything and we have decided that our path insists on our living now, not later, in the manner in which we would care (dare) to live, or at least as closely as is humanly possible in the given circumstances, we see immediately we are concerned with a question of quality. This is not merely in the area of aesthetics, though they come into it, but in the much wider one, embracing our inner lives as well as the outer, popularly referred to nowadays as the quality of life.

It is a phrase, this, a picture of what ought to be, which is not only a dream but a reflection of what most of us have experienced at some point or another as a fact and therefore a continuing possibility, which might appear to stand in very fragile relation with the realities today of our assorted politics of despair. This quality of life as the vision we attempt to live in every moment, in everything we are doing simultaneously with our heads, hearts and hands, *is* a tender plant. But that is why in the deserts of our days it becomes something so precious.

Quality: it has to be something we breathe and the reason why we do so.

Quality, let us make it clear, does not mean going around like a wet blanket, or a Goody Two Shoes. It means living skilfully, easily, by encountering each situation openly, fair-mindedly, then coming up with the appropriate response. Sometimes this does need to be fairly ruthless, as when one is called upon to be 'cruel to be kind'. There will be those occasions when we find there is no alternative but to stand up boldly to transgression and, metaphorically at least, swing a few punches. Quality also means, however, that when we ourselves fail to act in the appropriate way, skilfully, as we shall endlessly in moments of all too human dudgeon, sarcasm, whiplash anger and actions that do nothing for anyone, we have sufficient awareness to recognize the fact and make prompt amends by apologizing, proceeding to do what should have been done in the first place, and marking the error down yet again as another good lesson.

Quality understands that the more effectively we do handle ourselves, other people and situations that involve all of us, the easier, overall, the task becomes in one sense – proficiency improving with use – but more difficult in another. Our crudest errors, standing out like sore thumbs, we can detect and deal with fairly easily. But Quality knows that merely sandpapering our warts down is not quality. It is putting a face on things. Our deeper faults prove more resistant to daylight.

So Quality goes on honing us down even further.

The more clinically we start attacking long-established attitudes and systems of self-defence, however, the more something inside us is going to rebel. This part of us wants only to get on with surviving, having a good time and not having to put up with the dubious pother of 'self-improvement'. Eventually Quality, stripping us of layer after layer of self-pretence, all our vanities, wantings and thickly encrusted feelings of hurt and revenge, starts touching on some pretty raw nerves, and in trying to protect ourselves, cover up, there is a very real danger of our becoming extremely sophisticated in the new games we play with ourselves, thus creating delusions that end up more monstrous than anything with which we started.

Quality is dangerous.

Yet, it *is* interesting. In an age in which craftsmanship has been lost to most things, where we have turned to the jerrybuilt and the disposable as a way of life, whether one refers to goods, services or human beings and their relationships, the cultivation of Quality in our lives from the smallest act and feeling to the most important will in time, quite a surprisingly short one, instil in us a patience and pride which will make us realize how barren our lives had been without them.

This pride is not the kind that indulgently pats itself on the back. It is the feeling of accomplishment and wonder known to everyone who has pitted themselves against the odds, given all they have got, and found the outcome a widening of their understanding. It is the pride giving rise not to smugness but to joy.

In an era where most of us have become mere functionaries or button-pushers, it may be that the only real area left where there is scope any more for submitting to the learning and application and earning the psychological reward offered by craft skills, is working on ourselves. And in relating the importance of this work to the wider society and its future we might ponder the response of a master who when asked by a pupil what he needed to do to learn how to paint beautifully, replied, 'Make yourself beautiful, then paint naturally.'

Chapter 11
Transforming chores

Quality as something we bring to everything we do whatever the circumstances – how though can it come into the reckoning, practically speaking, if I am fortunate enough to have a job, but one which is absolutely ghastly and turning me into a zombie? Or how does one bring 'Quality' to any chore for that matter, such as having to clean out a filthy lavatory, wash my mouldering socks, or squeeze the boil on my neck?

Aren't we being a bit ambitious here?

To begin with let us appreciate that Quality does not mean we have to be superhumans who react to unpleasant tasks with wonderful imperturbability all the time, any more than it is realistic to expect ourselves to respond to sudden disaster with a skip and a dance.

It is appropriate and sensitive of us to blanch at foul jobs and unpleasant sights. Understandably it may be nicer to have work that involves travel to exotic places, and not to suffer from carbuncles. But there is nothing whatever in exotic locations or in the situation of being free of skin trouble that harbours intrinsic secrets of happiness, as consultation with a Trobriand Islander with a hangover or a human being with a clear complexion on Death Row will prove.

Chores are an inescapable part of all our lives. If these lives are to be made happy, the happiness will have to accommodate the chores somehow, once we have finished turning our noses up at them.

Quality is simply all about giving of our best. We 'care for' everything we do and hope to learn something from the task even if it does seem pointless or worthy only of our skimpiest response. It is a way of ensuring we approach every moment of our lives on as even a keel as possible . . . a balanced, just way of looking at what has to be done. It teaches us to approach life in an active and not merely a reactive fashion; stops us getting thrown when things do not go right.

If we see Quality as something we bring to some activities but not others we merely perpetuate the split world of desirable and despised experiences, and the more 'Quality' we might encounter in times of good fortune the more shabbiness and misery we are likely to meet when life goes sour on us, since the contrast proves too great.

So Quality has to be indivisible, like compassion; spread equally over all our actions and responses, otherwise it is likely to harm rather than benefit our purpose and prove not to be 'Quality' at all. Learning how to wash one's socks well and find the task instructive and pleasant is the sort of attention to fine detail which enables us eventually to piece together a considerable tapestry of such details and so make our lives as a whole well spent; that is, instructive and pleasant.

Quality is a thread that runs through everything, bringing together great and small and weaving a harmony out of them.

What Quality does here is really very simple. Acting as an unfailing guideline for all our endeavours, it sees we *make a habit* of doing things well so that we do not have to keep thinking twice about our attitude, wondering whether we should put a lot of ourselves into this activity (usually because we think we might get something out of so doing) and only a little into the other.

Usually our lives are full of bad habits of one sort or another (like only putting our backs into things that are to our apparent advantage . . .) which are all contributing factors to our unhappiness. Now, we try and reverse things.

Some of you might carp that if we put our backs into everything we do whether we enjoy doing it or not, we are going to end up exhausted. Life is tiring enough as it is, just 'coping' with it.

This kind of attitude betrays a certain ignorance again of the way energy works. What generates energy is our state of mind. If this is fed up with life, involved in a never-ending struggle with itself and all things, it stands to reason that body and soul are going to spend a lot of time feeling exhausted. If we see energy purely in physical terms, boredom – moping around without things to do – ought to give us plenty of spare energy to play with, but as anyone who has ever been bored or depressed knows, there can be few states more debilitating.

The fact is energy begets energy. Good energy leads to the good feelings – alertness, vitality and benevolence – which shape us up for happiness. And just as we try to make a habit of things like jogging or exercises to improve our wellbeing, so it makes sense to make a habit of the spontaneous mental attitudes directed to the same end.

But, you protest (scream?!), I am in this godawful dead-end post in which job satisfaction is precisely nil and my faculties are turning to pulp – how on earth can I practise 'Quality' in such a situation? There is no way I could ever bring myself to enjoy what I'm doing or kid myself that the end-product (bars of soap, rubber toy octopuses, income tax assessments; whatever) is of monumental importance to the enrichment of mankind, so what can I do?

There are four clear options open to you. First, you lump and like it. This, never forget, remains your *choice*: you are not, after all, employed in the Gulag. In time, applying what you know about the art of accepting things, you might arrive at a stoical acquiescence, a freedom from craving something else, you find quite restful. No more *chasing*!

Second, you can quit. Now. Here we decide that no job, no matter how secure and 'fortunate' with unemployment hitting the roof as it is, or well paid, is worth it finally if it drives us barmy. If we are that miserable at work we are going to be correspondingly miserable at home, and none of this is going to do very much for our relationships with our wives/husbands or loved ones and our children. So we shall try urgently to get other work which will give us more satisfaction even if it does mean a sacrifice (perhaps considerable too) of things like pay and status.

If we cannot find work we would like to do and our present job goes on undermining our entire existence, we have to think seriously about getting out anyway. We have to see whether we can trust life sufficiently to take a considerable risk, believing that we will not starve or come to grief altogether and that something will turn up somehow. Better to be out of work than out of one's mind. If you don't agree, your choice is clear. You stay where you are.

But between the extremes of submitting forlornly to one's

job and throwing it up even though you might have nothing with which to replace it, there are two other interesting avenues you might consider.

The first of these, our third grand option, is to accept that yes, I am 'stuck' in my present employment for one reason or another, but no, I am not going to go on accepting the way it is driving me into the ground. I have to do something about the way I relate to my work. I have to turn a dreary work-day into something better.

Certainly, one may have to accept that packing goods in cardboard boxes on an assembly line, or sitting in an office scratching away at double-entry bookkeeping, are not tasks that are going to reward you every day with an eight-hour rapture. The diversionary muzak droning away in the factory and the diversionary gossip droning away in the office are not ever going to divert your knowing deep down that fundamentally this kind of work is grotesque.

However, doing your work sloppily, living only for the milestone of the next tea-break, lunch-hour or whistle; letting everyone around you, colleague and employer alike, know in no uncertain terms how you loathe what you are doing and where you are; and perhaps even getting your own back on the rotten system that shackles you by deliberately sowing disgruntlement in the workplace or even going so far as to sabotage the work process – all these kinds of actions merely guarantee that the day grows longer along with the odds on your ever being able to feel happy at work.

If we give Quality a try, though, in the way we approach even the most eyeball-glazing task, we might be surprised by the outcome. We could for instance decide to pack our goods as carefully and efficiently as we can as a matter both of precision and pride, and we could have bursts of speeding up the operation considerably to make something of a game of the operation, testing our reflexes and staying power – basically doing no more than getting the blood going a bit so it does not degenerate into sludge, as it has a habit of doing in jobs like these. We do not sit or stand there in a glaze. We get stuck in.

The clerical work we might undertake with a craftsman's care, paying attention to the neatness of handwriting and layout so the completed page has a pleasant aesthetic feel about it; does not look as though it has been the route of a drunken spider dipped in ink . . . and of course making sure the figures do add up! Again we could have periods where we switch into intense concentration so we feel we are putting all of ourselves into the task to hand, even if it is lacklustre. We could do it *well*, forgetting our surroundings and all the sighs about what we might be doing if we didn't have to be here – the rat-babble of ifs, buts and maybes.

After these sustained immersions in the awfulness of what we are doing, it is likely we shall surface and discover the operation was not quite so awful after all. We might even feel a small glow of accomplishment. It is the experience again of losing oneself in the moment, the process of meditation-in-action during which we forget ourselves completely and become what we are doing. And it is the act of absorption itself, not in the least what it is that one happens to be absorbed in, which is all-important.

The human mind, awake, seems to thrive on this kind of activity more than anything else. It loves either to have to give itself to everything (utmost dedication to what has to be done) or to nothing (letting go quietly, say, in meditation). What it cannot abide is being led in several different directions at once. So if we are on the factory floor with a fraction of our minds given to the packing, a little bit more to the jingles from the loudspeakers, a further portion to fretting over the whole boring business and the largest share of all to doodling over what we might or might not be doing at the weekend, we must expect to find ourselves in the state commonly known as frazzled. This means experiencing ourselves as an untidy jangle of 'bits'.

Our bid for Quality does not have to stop, however, at bringing all these bits together in a sustained concentration on the task before us. Any workplace offers opportunities to extend the exercise of worth beyond this, especially in areas such as the relationships between ourselves and our colleagues and the not always easy association with our employer. This is not to suggest that we try to become 'yes men' to everyone. Far from it. The aim is to be people who are clearly their own man or woman at the same time as they are good team members genuinely interested in the lives and especially the difficulties of their fellow workers, and also to ensure the bosses themselves appreciate full well that *they* are being given nothing less than – Quality!

Looking, for the moment, outside ourselves in the search for job satisfaction – this leads to the fourth option open to us as we try to halt our slide and change our lives. If Option Three was about our deriving some sort of reward by changing our attitudes to whatever we do, Option Four decides to take a look at the operation itself and ponder if there might not be ways to make this more pleasant for everyone; of adapting our work to ourselves. We look at the idea of making changes in the way the job itself is done.

This asks that we get together intelligently with our colleagues and superiors and try to convince them that change would be both possible and beneficial. This admittedly can be the hardest part of any endeavour. But the areas where work might be altered to enhance job satisfaction are potentially enormous. The introduction of new working methods rather than technological processes is likely to be the most feasible proposition on the whole if immediate cost factors have to be borne in mind.

There could be new working partnerships or groupings on the factory floor, more worker participation in decision-making, the use of flexitime, imaginative incentive and recreation schemes, more civilized catering arrangements; a few improvements in the physical milieu – at any rate, *something*. And communication altogether could be lifted into a more open and constructive dimension by openness and constructiveness being taken straight to the management from the shop floor; the old, almost forgotten skills of taking the initiative!

Early on, for all kinds of reasons, the odds against you achieving anything might seem insuperable. But if you are determined enough to get something done to make this enforced surrender of five days of your seven to the Great God Work into at least a tolerable exchange, so that first thing Monday morning is not always the last thing you look forward to every week, organized sound ideas and the flying of imaginative kites from the workforce not only offer at least the possibility of a happier outcome for everyone, but the effort itself, opening up encouragement and interest all round, inevitably improves morale on the way.

If you surrender before you try your arm you have no moral right to complain about anything. Moaning, too, only drags one down further. Effort lifts us, and even if we fail and the job trundles on in its breathtakingly numbing fashion, it is not the end of the world. Our preoccupation with Quality ensures we gain something from the defeat. We do not let it quash us; we savour the satisfaction of at least having made a first-class effort. Then, if we still cannot abide the job as it stands, we have to go back and look again at our other options. There is an answer for us *somewhere*.

There always is.

Acceptance of things as they are, abandoning them, changing our attitudes towards them altogether or changing the circumstances themselves – the four options, if we look at them closely enough, offer more too than a solution of sorts to the problem of work and chores. They enable us to confront the many different kinds of difficulties most of us face nearly every day of our lives and work out a way of dealing with them. 'Quality' does not know defeat. It knows that if we give ourselves wholly to whatever we have to do we cannot help but learn how to be whole, and therefore happy.

Chapter 12
Mending our love lives

Along with work, what causes many of us our keenest unhappiness is the state of our relationship with our spouse or partner – the union of hearts and minds which was going to bring wholeness and happiness to our lives but which has invariably left us feeling more separate and down in the mouth than ever. Where do we go wrong?

The reasons we seek partners are many and complex, but the overwhelming impulse usually is to find someone who will compensate for what we are not and so 'complete' us. Very broadly, a man looks for a woman in order to bring what are traditionally described as feminine qualities into his life and a woman seeks a man to bring so-called masculine virtues into her own. It is this fundamental division, our incompleteness as individuals, which is supposed to be the drive behind the sexes coming together and procreating – producing more half-persons to keep the whole less-than-satisfactory cycle going. Creation myths around the world, however, speak of a time when it was host to races of rather happier, god-like, two-sexed creatures; though reproduction details tend to be hazy. Whatever; in the situation in which we find ourselves today, obviously we invest an enormous amount of psychological capital in the relationship with the person in whom we hope to 'find ourselves'.

A great deal is at stake.

But because it is, because we expect so much of our other halves, we are often in trouble from the start. All the freight we pile on our partners, all the freight they pile on us – it is small wonder that relationships which have as one of their desirable characteristics a feeling of 'lightness' find themselves staggering under an awesome weight even before they set off.

We subject our alleged loved ones to all kinds of pressures arising out of the rarely wholly stable history of ourselves; our neglect of self-knowledge. We make demands in conflict with one another's deepest requirements, or bent into retaliations and power games hardly calculated to do much for the health of any get-together.

Faced with these sorts of obstacles it is not surprising our relationships fail to surmount them in such abundance.

Understanding ourselves more, what we are really like, what we most seek in life, is important then if we are to stop the rot and have a union that does offer a hope of enlightening us and bringing us joy. We have to come up with ways to take the pressure off each other. And the most obvious one is to find a degree of wholeness within oneself that spares our having to live like a vampire all the time off our partner.

Short of our being saints or sages all of us are going to project our fantasies and overblown expectations on our loved ones to some extent and be in a position where we 'need' things from them, and there will be sizable tracts of interrelationship where we understand only dimly if at all what is going on; but if we start from the premise that finding a measure of our own completeness is one of the most likely guarantees of some success in a relationship, we are again being positive by taking responsibility for ourselves in our quest for fruitful life.

Also, in seeking to spare our partners as much of our psychological rubbish as possible and give them the space and autonomy to cultivate their own completeness, we are behaving immediately in a considerate, compassionate manner, and such qualities being the classic foundations of all relationship, we are getting off to a first-class start.

This kind of sensitivity to our companions and what passes between us is nourished especially by the exercise at all times of total honesty (in so far as one is able to be 'totally' honest when we lack the wisdom to see all things), and keeping open lines of lively communication. It is remarkable and saddening to survey relationships and discover so many where unconditional honesty is not seen as a prerequisite of happiness, or to note how often it happens that a couple cannot or will not talk gently and constructively with each other in an effort to resolve their difficulties.

How often do we encounter people saying they would rather not know, thank you, if their partner was sleeping with someone else, or that they would not dream of letting them know their most intimate secrets? How often do we hear the grim silences lasting months and years, or the dialogues degenerating endlessly into arid conventions, or into anger and tears?

But if we cannot live together in frank exposure to each other, with nothing hidden and therefore no games to play in hiding things, the prospects of our finding anything remarkable in our union are snuffed out rather early. If we subscribe to a relationship which tolerates untruth and half-truth and we cannot sit down with our partners to share our deepest feelings with each other in order to learn how to overcome estrangement and hurt by dropping pride and resentments; cannot reach out to the other person with our caring as a matter of course; we might be said to be not so much people sharing a journey, an adventure, as two stuffed parrots in a cage.

Ever since the early 1960s we have been inundated with sex manuals telling us how we can 'save' our marriages and love matches – get transported as far as the Hesperides even – by tweaking this appendage or that orifice, or ravelling ourselves in fancy positions, but what these sticky tomes invariably fail to do is spell out the quiet, beautiful truth that the most fantastic thing we can ever do in our love lives is to hug someone gaily (yes, as though we would become them), be able to say 'I love you' whilst looking them deep in the eye, and know how to say 'I'm sorry' when the time is right. This is art. The rest is mechanics.

But we can only have these sublime skills when we know basically what it is to love as distinct from handing out what commonly passes for the gift and turns it into sly theft. Love expects nothing, it is as they say sufficient unto itself. And therefore it can only be given in the fullest sense by those, too, who are 'sufficient unto themselves'; that is whole, or aiming that way – those who are not using relationships as props for their inability to handle life on their own, or for their status requirements, or the plethora of different reasons men and women seek to come together in peace but end up instead in the sex war.

A good way to kick off a relationship that might be free of the common guerilla activities is for each person to confess to the other that there *is* selfishness attached to the love on offer, mutually exploring their needs and expectations, then to make a commitment to pursue creatively not only their personal and joint interests but also a higher understanding together of what it is to – love. 'We are flawed, needy, and shall use each other for a long time, but we'll work hand in hand to try and go beyond need and "use", and see what lies there.'

If a couple can approach each other with this kind of awareness and ambition, each party is able then to act as a guide or teacher for the other. This is not a matter of pulling each other up all the time, rubbing the other's snout in their faults, though 'correction' of a gentle kind will enter the reckoning to some extent, but more important, talking through one's problems as amicably as possible as a spontaneous way of living together, with the accent neither on blaming the other nor oneself; instead, on learning to understand the reasons we act the way we do.

If little by little we can learn to come to each other without blame, justification or any of the various subtle ploys we have nearly all used to try to make ourselves feel good on the strength of the other person's being made to feel bad, which if one thinks about it is not only unlikely to do very much for the relationship either now or later but also amounts to a species of sadism, we might begin to have a partnership worthy of the name.

Cleansing ourselves of the worst projections with which couples regularly bespatter each other, we shall find each partner is able then to act as a very useful mirror to the other and the relationship will thrive on the exchange of positive and often fascinating realization which must result. Most relationships start to rot when people feel stuck in them, but if we are enjoying a constant diet of revelation and surprise about

    a) ourselves,
    b) the person we have chosen to live with and
    c) the two of us as a team,

we are involved in an energetic process of growth, and even if this is painful and destabilizing sometimes it would never do to describe it as *boring*.

It is relationships we have formed as refuges against the world or as buttresses for our whole being which become that.

These are the sort of marriages and liaisons we think will spare us the pain of being alive. We see them as anodynes; protections against rather than propulsions into new experiences. But all attempts to erect a shelter round one's ears and get another person plugged into our psyches like a dripfeed are perilous to our happiness for a number of reasons.

On one level we just find ourselves stagnating. On another, growing and moving on whether we like it or not, we watch horrified as the dreariness of stagnation starts to fragment as do the foundations of a house being undermined by an underground torrent and, literally, we start to crack up. Then when this happens we see that our life support system, our partner, either does not support us because there is a limit to the extent anyone else can be for us what we are not − fill in for our inadequacies − or has decided he or she is sick of stagnation and neurosis and has fled anyway. Hereabouts, our lives having been taken away from us because we never claimed them for our own, we start to experience the terror of total failure, total loss. Heigh ho our nervous breakdown!

Because of our inadequacies there will be times when we shall behave badly towards each other despite our best intentions. We shall be angry with each other, know hurt and resentment, sometimes ponder whether it might not be better to end the relationship and perhaps even experience moments in it of futility and great despair. But if we have been serious so far about our commitment of care and understood the importance of Quality, and have taken upon ourselves that power of the alchemist/magician who can dissolve a tear into sunlight, we shall find there is nothing, nothing, that can stand in our way. We cannot do other, still, than move on, to love.

A good way to keep the whole process alive is for the pair of you to agree formally that no matter how fiercely you might have been at loggerheads during the day, even up to the point you are going to bed at night, you will never allow the quarrel or unspoken pique to be carried over to the following day. You will settle your difference in friendship before you sleep. Every new day to start with a new slate. That is your promise to each other, and perhaps the only marriage vow ever worth the breath.

You could reinforce the agreement with a penalty system,

because there will be times almost certainly when you will not make up and mend, instead subsiding into bed with backs poignantly glaring at each other or the two of you behind slammed doors in separate rooms – your wisdom and wonderful marriage-saving schemes in tatters, Carruthers.

Penalties could be that in a case where you have one partner spurning late-night conciliation, he or she is obliged then to take the other out to supper the following evening or on the first suitable occasion, or if nights on the town are not feasible for economic or parental reasons, or are not your idea of fun, to be responsible for giving the other some little surprise during the day.

If such devices fail and the dispute smoulders on day after day, night after night, with one partner still refusing to abide by the rules, then you have a sliding scale of fines, say 25p or £1 (or a dollar or two) the second night, 50p or £2 the third and so on, which the recalcitrant spouse has to pay when he or she has finally melted and started speaking again, so the innocent party or perhaps we should say the flexible one ends up with an evening out and a little pocket money to their credit.

In the case where neither of you plays the game, both keeping the war going for some time, you will share the costs of a night out or some treat when the rift is healed, and the fines you have notched up together you will lob into a charity or some such deserving cause. So, every time, the dark is finally made to give way to the light; to something useful.

Some of you might feel these are just absurd gimmicks having little to do with the long hard graft of two people learning how to live together in the face of some of the hazards confronting coupledom or family life today. But it is precisely because the road is long and hard for most of us that we do try to lighten it with ideas like these, looking wherever possible for opportunities to be creative and stimulating, simply different from the sagging norms, in the relationships we are trying to build.

That said, the greatest safety-valve or truly creative act remains our ability to take our partners in our arms and tell them we are sorry and that we love them; that we want to make something rare and beautiful out of our being together. Even if we are not uncomplicated enough to be able to do something so simple, whatever we might do even in a roundabout way to convey feelings of this kind and hasten such a conclusion, is an act noble and good, so cannot fail to further the cause of life.

We help ourselves grow more whole and less of an imposition on our partner by also steering clear when we can of the stereotypes in which it is so easy to lock ourselves in dependencies. If I see myself as the archetypal, stiff-upper-lipped, breadwinning male and you see yourself as the consummately 'weepie' wife and mother, we are going to need each other pretty badly to make up for the other half of experience almost totally lacking in our orbit as individuals. Unless I am able to experience within myself to some useful degree what it is like to be female and if you do not remotely know what it is to be male, the amount of empathy and sympathy we are able to extend to each other is bound to be limited, and in relating to a partner across a huge divide we make it much more unlikely we will ever come together in a fruitful 'whole'. Macho men and baby dolls must always remain miles apart.

Men looking after the children for part of the time and women going out to work likewise, and exchange of traditional 'male' and 'female' responsibilities generally, an increasingly popular accommodation these days, will possibly help the process of identifying with the lot of our partner and his or her sex as a whole, but there is always the danger here of perpetuating conceptualization anyway – 'role reversal' still means we see life in terms of roles, and life teaches us that if we do that we merely spend it ricocheting from one to the other, other, expanding our energy unnecessarily in trying to prove one role or way of life (argument, philosophy, etc.) is better than another instead of ridding oneself of fixed ideas altogether (including the idea of 'no fixed ideas' of course) and learning what it is to live.

Fixed divisions of labour or responsibility or attitudes assigning mysterious superiority to one of life's unavoidable tasks over another are anathema to the process of cultivating wholeness, freedom and love. In a wise relationship in a contemporary culture freed of the necessity to be either one thing or the other, each partner does not have to deliberate in the least, as a major issue, on 'who does what'. Each partner lends an equal hand to whatever has to be done, whenever, so the couple engage in a constantly evolving overlap of energy and interest in which all constructs and labels attempting to link identity with set ways of doing or looking at things simply fade.

If a situation for a majority of the time is such that one partner has to work and the other look after children, obviously a choice involving 'division' has to be made, but whoever does what regards neither option as being of more value intrinsically than its 'opposite'. Both are necessary. Both are good.

Bringing up a child to be happy in this world is as important and rewarding a task as getting elected to office or driving a bus.

Men and women who feel reasonably secure and whole are therefore able to enjoy a rich variety of experiences and responses within their relationship, and since variety is supposed to be the spice of life we can add excitement to the list of virtues of empathy and understanding which must always help the sexes in their long struggle to come together.

If partners freewheel in their liaison, and going out to work, bathing baby, doing the shopping, mending a fuse, cooking, settling the bills, telling bedtime stories, fixing social arrangements and making love are not the prerogative of either one, but of both according to circumstances or inclination, then they are not likely to have the *time* to feel hemmed in and bored beyond redemption and will learn to stop seeing themselves less as institutionalized men and women and more as free (complete) human beings.

Such freedom means that when we do then submit to the ultimate nakedness of making love we do not have to keep trying furiously to put up defences all the time to protect a vulnerability which has been fed on stereotypes always threatening us with our failure to live up to them. I do not have to play the bull male, you do not have to ape the swooning siren: we can be whatever we want to be. We can play. We can explore. Dammit, we can do what one is meant to do with sex, *enjoy* it!

If I do not need you to prove my masculinity to myself

because I feel secure enough in it as it is and therefore do not need to prove it to you either, I can allow the feminine in me to have its say also in the love-making; altogether be relaxed and creative about the whole enterprise, which is far more likely to make for shared enjoyment than if each of us has to 'prove' ourselves on our partner. This way we do not have to 'rape' our partners to wrest a fleeting completeness out of them. Instead, we float.

If orgasms frenetically arrived at are the only moments in our lives when we do manage to escape from the prisons of ourselves, we may be fine athletes but we are spiritual beggars. And all the sex aids in the world cannot compensate for the fact we do not know how to love.

All the 'problems' we may encounter in our sex lives, such as boredom, impotence, frigidity, what people like to call perversion – you name it – are able to be treated in time with the exercise of this the supreme gift. Relaxation, tenderness and humour, all of which are vehicles of it, are not beyond the purview of the majority of us. Slowly, having an orgasm which blows your head off ceases to have its old importance and when this happens the more the likelihood, by chance (apparent though of course not so), that we shall experience an orgasm which does have the neighbours banging on the walls.

To be able to experience this kind of love does not necessarily mean we have to be hooked into a passionate affair with someone. Such would rarely amount to love anyway, more a tropical disease. The love which heals is more to do with gentleness and compassion; with embracing partners in such a way that they are able perhaps for the first time in a long time, even in their lives, to surrender all their worries and fears by sinking into your arms and the warmth they offer, *in trust*. At last they have found a space into which they can let go. They know they have nothing to fear from us; nothing either to defend or fight. They are able to be themselves.

Enabling others to be the people they are, or might be, is the supreme goal of love; the greatest act of 'liberation' we can know.

Even if I still have trouble keeping erect, or you continue to have a problem reaching orgasm, or we find it beyond us to copulate six times a week swinging from the chandelier or doing it upside down in the broom cupboard; while we may require one or two blowzy fantasies to keep the juices running and the limbs willing – none of this really matters two hoots either way if we are able to open our hearts to each other and become the sweet ways of talking and touching, laughing and joshing, which steer us ineluctably towards the dropping of all barriers which is the secret of love.

This is the undivided article which cares as much for the beggar in his dark, the way we prepare our humble bowl of soup or listen to the wind in the trees, as for the man or woman in our arms. And every human being is potentially capable of it.

You can reach out to your partner right now and advance farther still in this long, unwinding way to truth. You can tell them there is nothing in the whole world you want to be able to do more than – care.

Whether your partner then comes to meet you halfway does not concern you at this point. You have done what you had to do, what was skilful. As for your 'reward', you care sufficiently about the giving not to care.

Time, as well as 'nothing', brings all things.

Go to your loved one. Approach the partner who, sadly, has become a stranger in your midst. Go humbly even to the husband or wife you have come to hate the sight of.

Beyond this there is nothing more to do.

Chapter 13
Parenthood without pressure

Many of us try to advance our happiness through our children. We should not be astonished therefore that so many of our offspring end up unhappy, and ourselves with them.

From the word 'go' they have to carry such a burden of responsibility for us.

While the reasons for our conceiving children will range from the sublime to the ridiculous down to the accidental, their arrival in a sorrowing world is more often than not greeted with a hope of some kind that they might come to act as a hedge against it. In the East, impoverished parents sometimes mutilate their children physically so that, eliciting maximum pity, these might beg more successfully and support the family into old age; and elsewhere, regularly, we tend to do something not dissimilar with our children on a psychological level. All too often we use them (if surreptitiously) for our own ends first.

We want them to be images of ourselves, mirrors to our vanities. If we are rich and famous we want these offspring to carry on the family name in the grand manner. If we are poor and unknown we would like our children to compensate for our lack by doing something . . . in the grand manner. We mutilate them to feed our egos if not our stomachs.

So from the start we are concerned not so much with the child's unique, individual development as with his or her being 'successful'. This we fondly believe will make for happiness all round. But whatever we do to mould infants to our whims, fancies or deepest needs, we beggar them to the degree we deny them scope to develop, find, themselves. Some children, with unusual gifts, will always overcome the handicaps of birth and upbringing to become luminaries of one sort or another. But many with more modest aptitudes will suffer under the inducements to become this, that or the other at variance with what they have the potential of being, and a nature out of kilter, whether it learns to become 'successful' or not, must always by definition be unnatural and unhappy.

Nearly all of us have so lost our way in understanding what it is to be natural, we have scant idea any longer, if we ever did have in the mass, of the best way to bring up our children and promote the mutual happiness of the generations. After the old harsh ways of the stick and carrot we have tried a much different approach in the past three decades. Discipline has been countered with licence even here. Schools which set one child against another have been succeeded by institutions where the very ideas of demarcation and competition are despised, if rarely lived to the letter. Parents have tried not to be parents but 'friends'. Authority has been sensitive about being seen to be such. But whether they get the gospel ancient or modern, young people continue to grow up above all with doctored minds and undernourished hearts.

Since we send children today into a world of spent but enduringly antagonistic ideologies and ethical decay, with a future largely offering economic duress, social instability and worse, efforts to fit our wards securely into the systems responsible for the shambles, so they can be 'happy' and we might rejoice on the proceeds, are logically inept from the start.

The sensible debate we should be having with ourselves is not whether we ought to send our child to this school or that one, encourage it into this trade or that profession, or get it to follow any one set lifestyle at the expense of another, but how do we equip it with the very special qualities that are going to be needed by individuals in the years ahead if they are not to subsist nihilistically on a diet of fear and hopelessness. The most important thing we can nurse in this beleaguered generation against all the odds is a self-generating love of life that would enable a person to find reason for living even in great hardship, at the same time as it impelled him to commit himself to the wider fight against darkness irrespective of the personal cost.

The emphasis ought not to be on 'making it' and 'faking it' but on the growth of courage and independence; what not all that long ago we liked to call 'character' but which is a goal that has gone out of fashion among both parents and teachers when it comes to bringing up children. Being popular, getting good exam results, degrees, promotions and glory are all seen as infinitely more desirable prizes than the slow purchase of integrity and wisdom.

Education like this, however, ensures that child and parent see happiness only in terms of attainment, a happiness dependent on something outside itself, so we condemn both them and us to lives of anything but contentment – unless either of us is fortunate enough at some point along the line to see the light and realize what needs to be done to change things.

The greatest thing we can ever do for the happiness of our children is have no expectations of them. None.

This does not mean we don't care what happens to them. Exactly the opposite; we care so much that we refuse to subject them to the intolerable pressures being put on them these days by parents motivated more by fear and ambition than by love.

One does not doubt that parents who drive, coerce and indoctrinate their children do so, even while they are being selfish in the process, 'with the best of intentions' too. They want their sons and daughters to survive and be spared hardship, at the very least. The world it seems grows a more insecure and desperate place every year. The 'weak' are going to the wall in droves. It makes sense to try to equip our children with the strength – the skills and protections we like to believe provide this – which will see to it that they keep their heads above water. It's not a world for 'lofty idealism', one regrets to say. Facts have to be faced. And so on, and on.

But this approach not only makes our young people highly *vulnerable to* rather then protected against whatever setbacks lie in the years ahead, since rigid conformity has scant value in a topsy-turvy world, it does not do much either for their happiness right now.

Children have enough pressure on them outside family life as it is. The demands of their schools and the enticements and distortions of the media, shrinking futures from shrinking job markets, the considerable and not always enlightened influences of other children and *their* parents, the shoddy ethical leadership offered generally in the adult world – children are battered from every quarter. The majority of them then come home to be 'battered' by their parents. There seem to be few areas where they can find relief from the bombardment, the anxiety.

The home should surely be the one place at least where they find this? We the parents ought to be the ones lightening the load, not increasing it.

Competing with so many external influences, the parents' task of offering alternative values and ideas to their children, freely, is never going to be an easy one. On the other hand if we do have the good sense to make the domestic milieu a haven from pressure, its contrast with the disconcerting reality of the outside world is likely to make it not only a healthy relief but also an attraction. The child will have some 'measure' he can work with to help him develop his own ideas of what he wants and needs. We give him space in which he can open out and grow.

There does not seem much of value we can teach our children anyway other than by quiet example. There is enough evidence to hand now that trying to fashion them according to fine theoretical blueprints is counter-productive, the children of conventional parents regularly going off to be drop-outs for instance and the offspring of drop-outs growing up to be stalwarts of suburbia. There is nothing uncanny about this. If I have been shaped fiercely in one way, my innate self-correcting yen for wholeness inevitably leads me to try to shape *myself* in the alternative area of experience with which I am hopelessly unfamiliar. If I am set on rearing my daughter as a feminist it might be better if I brought her up to become a nice little housewife and mother. When (we need to remind ourselves constantly) I am pushed from one direction, I fall in the other.

The 'right way' to bring up a child is not either by the strictly disciplined approach or allowing the creature to do what it wants when it wants all the time. There can be no 'right way' since if there was we would not be inhabiting a world today in which we are forced to deal with so much that has gone wrong. In so far as the word means a technique or ideology there is no known 'way' we can rear our children. If someone claimed to have invented one they would also have to claim they were the Almighty.

Since we have no textbook to guide us we are thrown back, not for the first time, on experience. No one has been able to show yet that the mass of murderers, villains and derelicts come to be that way via childhoods which offered them love and the psychological security said to go with it. There is a great deal of evidence to link such unfortunates with childhoods of indifference and brutality, broken homes and hearts.

Regimented disciplinarianism and *laissez-faire* having come up with no coherent lessons from their opposition, and the only lesson to hand being that great misfortune and unhappiness are usually the product of loveless childhoods, good sense sees that love of the kind we have been looking at on this journey appears the most useful asset we can bring to parenthood that wants to be reasonably certain of doing some good.

Since this love is a gift, not an object of exchange and mart, or pressure, and this is the gift of 'letting be', of allowing others to be the people 'they are or might be', such parenthood cannot be an attempt to impose anything on anyone. We cannot force our love on our children, instruct them didactically in any set way, because if we do we are not *giving* them our love.

This might appear a good argument for the libertarianism which has been tried extensively of late but still left us with a young generation that is anything but 'free'. 'Letting be', however, is not an abnegation of responsibility, allowing a child to behave consistently in whatever way it desires. If a child grows up believing it can do that with impunity it is obviously heading for disaster. It would not be 'love' to let him or her sail blithely into such pitfalls. It would be the imposition of a misguided '-ism'. Love, like freedom, involves the constant exercise of responsibility.

It is neither love nor freedom to allow a child to burn its hand in the fire.

It is an advantage to the child as an innocent abroad to learn what exercising this responsibility amounts to, and its importance to itself and the society of which it is part. To some extent therefore it obviously needs instruction. But if as happens frequently this comes in one form or another as a moral code blithely wafted about in lip service but widely ignored in practice not just in the world at large but all too often at home, the child finds instruction in little other than confusion and cynicism.

Because the quality of public manners and ethics leaves so

much to be desired, the importance of the quality we bring to such in the home, in our intimate relationships, is all the more considerable if these are to be instrumental in any shaping of a better world. The best hope the child will have of coming to muster the courage and insight which will spare his descent into the common wilderness and unhappiness will derive from his having experienced the real possibility of an alternative. The first and finest access to that possibility, if not always the final one, is to be had through parental example. Their knowing there *is* another way – this alone is all we need to bequeath to our children.

So there is no 'way' to teach the child, there is only a way to live, letting the other make up his or her own mind about it in relation to what popularly goes by the name of living in the world outside. You give the child freedom to choose, secure in the knowledge born of experience that by the time he needs to, he is more likely than not then to know what choosing freedom is. You can do no more.

Meanwhile you most certainly do not want your offspring to be the university degree you never had, a famous barrister, husband of a beautiful wife with 2.2 children, two homes and 1.7 motor cars; provider of the grandchildren who'll give you something to wrap yourself around in your old age; all kinds of wonderful things to brag about to the neighbours and the general feeling that you, Muggins, have made quite a coup of your life. You just want him to be himself and happy; no more.

And in trying to lead him to the years where he might uncover these treasures for himself there will be times I am sure when it will be helpful to him if I am a disciplinarian. Situations are almost certain to arise, even, when I shall be tempted to resort to physical punishment, but since – if we can pause here to remind ourselves – he who resorts to violence in order to win an argument has already lost it, it will be wiser to seek more skilful ways of assisting the child to grow. But yes, I shall be stern, very, when the occasion demands.

Then, when it also demands, I shall let him do what he wants to even though I think his choice unwise, since if it is so, he will find out soon enough and thereby learn more effectively than if he had merely been subjected to parental whinge. All the time, he will be encouraged to make his own choices. In dress, pastimes, friends, schooling and career, he decides. I will guide if necessary or asked to do so, prompt, and sometimes disagree strongly, but only interfere if his choices threaten grave hurt to himself and others – if for instance he teamed up with muggers for a hobby or took to raiding post offices for a living.

Otherwise all I do is love him and let him go, just as one seeks to let go of everything that egotism keeps insisting we possess.

Because I am not trying to make him into anything he is not already (if he did not have a predisposition towards being a barrister no amount of my bullying would make him into an effective and, more important, a happy one), only trying to give him the room and encouragement to find and develop his potential, I am not likely to bedevil our relationship with anxiety. This in turn can only help him be less anxious and able to cope better with the complexities of growing up. All round I enjoy myself more, too.

Naturally most grown-ups will worry for their children at least some of the time, but how often do we hear a young person pleading exasperatedly with its parents, 'Look, will you please stop worrying about me, I'm *all right*!'? Often. The fact is children and young people, being supple of mind and spirit still as well as in body, are often able to deal with complications and setbacks more successfully than we sometimes care to admit. Our own fussings and frettings usually only make things worse for them.

What we can best do time and again is simply 'be there' for the child when he or she is overwhelmed by events and does need comfort and a helping hand. We have to relate to the child in such a way that it knows without even having to deliberate about it that we can be relied upon to be a real friend and ally when the need arises. It is no use telling either boy or girl that they should come to us whenever they are in trouble, that we are always ready to help them, if their experience of us has itself usually amounted to a lot of trouble.

Trust, like love or freedom, cannot be imposed; it has to be earned. And a child who has suffered parents who constantly nag, dictate to, bribe and threaten it is still going to be on the defensive – indeed more so – when suddenly they begin to break out in smiles and come 'bearing gifts'.

He or she knows we are uptight. Knows that no matter how pretty our disguises, basically we (like children) always want things to go our way.

This understood, we are not likely to endear ourselves to our children and do much for the happiness of either them or us if we are bending over backwards all the time to accommodate them and be 'mates' rather than parents. The trendy parent trying hard to be as contemporary as its offspring, living in a never-ending terror of the accusation he might be old-fashioned and out of touch, has been with us in some numbers since the mid-1960s, even if these are beginning to decline somewhat in the more realistic years of late, but studies have shown that adults who behave like this do not earn the trust and admiration of the young so much as their contempt. Children like to relate to people who act their age but do not use it as an exercise of power.

The exercise of great love will provide us with all the 'power' and authority, together with the understanding and kindness, we shall need.

As with my lover, where the child and I are most likely to free each other from anxiety and enrich each other's lives will be in the way we talk together, and here as the parent I bear much responsibility. I have to fulfil my express function as such. Not many families seem to know how to talk well among themselves; usually there are so many games being played just below the surface that communication inevitably becomes as wary as a walk through a minefield. This of course is so conducive to increased resentment and tension it can virtually be guaranteed that something will blow up eventually.

Time is of the essence once more: if as in so many cases these days we simply do not devote sufficient of it to sitting down and chewing the fat with one another, we can hardly be expected to develop conversation to the point where it does what more than anything else it is intended to do – bring people together in mutual understanding and promote the security and happiness of the race.

We end up as we do in oh so many instances, language blowing around the room like winter leaves.

Everyone likes to blame the sheer pace of life now for so much of what is wrong with it, not least the decline of the tradition of the family hearth and the way this used to bring families together, in theory at least. But the fact is we have more leisure now than ever, and in an age where the individual is so buffeted in the outside world we often look upon home as more of a harbour than ever, too; yet it is not conversation which fills these long sweet hours of domestic freedom, nor usually what makes even a minimal impact on them – it's TV, video, stereos, the kids up in their dens, Dad behind the paper, Mother sighing somewhere in between and the most animated dialogue in the house coming from the pet budgerigar and its glass reflection in the corner.

When we do talk it is about what happened at school or work, what's on the box, who's up to what in the neighbourhood, what we must get when we go shopping, how we'll spend our holidays in the summer, why we can't afford new curtains and, endlessly, What's Best For The Kids – and it is small wonder that children whose interior universes are resplendent with towering feelings, $64,000 questions, deep insights and invariably no little 'great love', sit mentally raising their eyebrows to heaven wondering why it is, *why*, that parents give the appearance they know everything at the same time as they seem to see nothing. It is not a bad question.

But the child will not tolerate this insufferable desert. He *will* ask questions. He will demand that the parents give him their time, give of themselves. Desperately he will try to belong to this so-called family unit just as he tries so hard to belong to everything else at this stage since he is still not free of the womb. However, then what happens?

'Why d'you come up with such ridiculous questions?', 'Go ask your father', 'I haven't time to sit and listen to your whimperings, dear', 'Another time, darling', 'Don't your teachers tell you these things?', 'I dunno', 'Could be', 'Really?' – such are the linguistic delights with which we bedazzle the sensibilities of millions of our children.

Then when we are conscientious, when we do aspire to being one big happy family, what is our idea of 'togetherness' usually? *Doing things.* Shopping together, building bookshelves together, going boating together, camping together, playing electronic games together and of course watching that TV together. But if in the midst of all this wonderful shared activity the child never comes to experience the 'heart to heart' which is the dialogue of true togetherness, of opening ourselves to one another as gifts, the contrast between all this physical proximity and psychological distance will increase and the youngster come to feel more isolated and unhappy than ever.

When this contrast settles into being a way of life, without relief, the offspring gives up on home. Altogether. If these parents of his are the sort of people he is destined to become – no thank you, brother. Nothing makes sense because at home no one ever talked either excitement or sense. They lived and conversed like robots.

And a new generation grows up to converse with fruit machines, space invaders, graffiti, slogans, grunts and knives. Or, if they are from a better class of background, with flummery rolling off forked tongues.

As every counsellor knows, the art of helping people to be happy is above all the art of listening. It is not even in the smallest degree a matter of laying down the law, or even instructing the other person to go in this direction or that. To be happy we have to have inner autonomy, be able to think and act for ourselves, so all attempts to 'meddle' in our lives will do more damage than good. To be able to think and act independently we need first to be able to stand back a sufficient distance to observe the full range of the choices before us, and second, to have been brought up or taught in such a way that we can know in our hearts which of these *is* for us. Our gift as parent to child is to provide the space and the heart.

To do this we have to have the space and heart ourselves; we need to be happy. It is an awesome responsibility. But if we are fully aware of it, the funny thing is it does not feel like one at all.

Chapter 14
The illusion of security

And when the children have flown, what then? A new unknown opens before us. We feel the ground shift under our feet a bit, a cooler breeze blowing round our ears. We are getting older. We feel afraid.

Even if we have had what we like to think of as a reasonably happy life so far and acquired a certain know-how in maturity, we start to ponder if all this still couldn't vanish as night comes on. What happens if we end up lonely old souls – senile?

If we look back with a sharp eye, however, we shall see that throughout our lives we have always been troubled by change, first the threat of it and then the invariably uneasy passage of it. It is usually this which has caused us more unhappiness than anything. Just as soon as we reckon we have achieved something or got somewhere in life, what happens? The rug gets pulled from under us.

Alas, there is no escape. Even if we lived in times of great peace and money grew on trees, we would still have the problem. The life of the human being, whatever his fate, is irrevocably a matter of change; about ten wholly new atomic compositions of ourselves in the average (Western) lifespan for instance. Then there is the little matter of the seven ages of man, or his vaunted seven-year life cycles, the so-called five crises and the two periods of his life when he is likely to feel the ground is not merely shifting under his feet but opening up in yawning chasms under him, around the late twenties and early forties, when it is said serious disorder and even breakdown are particularly likely to occur. All in all then, a dizzying business.

It is easy enough in times of economic hardship and dwindling expectations to understand why people try to turn in on themselves, clinging more fondly than ever to home, their few possessions, a not particularly appetizing but at least a fairly safe job, and to boring but faintly anaesthetizing routines.

We watch TV and see the terrible lives people are leading in the Third World and the terrible lives a good many people are even being forced to live in our own, and we shudder, hug the fire and thank heaven for small mercies. At least we have *something* to hang on to.

Then perchance we walk out of the door and nearly get run down by a bus. We miss death by a hair's breadth. Life, it maybe starts to dawn on us, is so incredibly fragile.

And there is no such thing as security, anywhere. Nothing we can hang on to.

Really, that can be quite a relief.

For if happiness cannot be found by burrowing away for it like a demented mole, nor certainty about one's fate be had from any quarter, and security in life while it lasts is only an absurd illusion fostered by vested interests such as building societies, insurance companies and promoters of the work (slave) ethic; then logically the lives we spend in such turmoil trying to possess these things are, broadly speaking, farces – wastes of the considerable time and energy that go into turmoil; resources which would be better invested in something far more creative and life-affirming.

Observe the problem. Life.

This, like the river, is flowing along in its familiar wild, choppy way, dashing itself on rocks and either pouring over them or parting and going round them, always following the curves of the land and seeking the line of least resistance; above all in zestful mien as it keeps its destiny, via ceaseless change, with its death and fulfilment, the sea. But what do *we* do?

We squat on the bank marvelling at all the flying spray and rainbows and energy of it all, the sheer excitement, and because we have been taught to acquire things as a way of 'finding' them we say 'Yes, this is a wonderful thing before me, I want to be part of it', and promptly stick our bucket over the edge and grab a few gallons for ourselves.

Then we pour our find into a shallow hole we have prepared in the ground. We make a small pond. This is *my* river-of-life. *My* effort to find happiness and meaning.

I might then stick a pretty little house on the pondside and use the water to irrigate some flowers and shrubs. I might stock it with a few trout and go out on it a lot in my rowboat, lying idly on my back with a line over the side and gazing up contentedly at the clouds. Everything begins to feel good. Captivated by my happiness, and maybe my spread, a good-looking woman moves in with me. I feel *terrific*.

I've carved out a small portion of paradise for myself.

But after a while what happens is that the water starts to turn murky, and smell. There is nothing flowing either into it or out. Then, rapidly, the whole pond goes stagnant. It fills with choking weeds you cannot row through any more that kill all the fish. Finally the waterhole starts to dry up altogether, disappearing into the ground. The surrounding greenery shrivels. I get ratty. My woman gets ratty. Life in the grand little paradise begins to taste of dust.

We have paid the price of trying to create a happiness for ourselves alone. Of trying to arrest the natural flow of life instead of jumping into it and seeing where it might take us.

To be able to 'go with the flow' means to cope with change, to accept security's illusion. At its best too it does not only mean coping with the change after it has occurred, learning something from it. We do not just want to be wise after the event, raking through the ashes as it were. More important, we want to transform difficult experience into something tolerable *even at the point it overtakes us*.

Up to now, learning how to deal with misfortune, we have largely been concerned with *faits accomplis*. In time we can perhaps come to terms with most things – unemployment, broken romances or whatever – but now we are going to move on: what we are going for is the ability to ride the setbacks, almost gaily, *now*. The moment they happen. This is speeding up our process of alchemical transformation with a vengeance!

We want to handle our reverses in such a way that we do much to overcome them before they build up into a catalogue of calamity. This is skill of a very high order; an attempt to avoid the many great misfortunes that are the sum of our own making, as well as withstanding, on the spot, the ones which are not.

Artistic geniuses have usually proved to be reasonably good at this kind of transmutation; despair, even, giving rise to extremely powerful waves of sweet feeling, poetic inspiration, as it is contended with on canvas or page. But one does not have to be either artist or genius to be able to do this conjuring trick. I just have to practise losing some of my isolating sense of 'me' and feel the bewilderment and pain not as my own especially but as the common experience of the human race. A trouble shared with someone is a trouble halved, so one which we can perceive as being the lot of all men, many of whom will be stricken even more severely than we are, is likely to lose quite a lot of its potency since the hold of the ego, which is that which feels assault most keenly, is itself diminished.

We breathe deeply, and if it looks as though we are going to be dashed on the rocks in this 'river of life', perhaps it is time for the cheering black joke about the worst that can happen to us in this corporeal caper being that we can 'snuff it'. Not such a shocking thing when you think about it; it is going to happen anyway. Truly, the worst aspect about anything invariably turns out to be not so much the event itself as the worrying about it. As Auden put it:

In headaches and in worry
Vaguely life leaks away.

Next, we look, hard, at what is happening to us. And we vow to find *something* positive in the mess.

Your wife has just walked out on you, suddenly you have been given your cards at work, someone has gazumped you on the house you have set your heart on buying, or your teenage daughter has announced she is pregnant. Each a kick in the stomach; an abrupt and sickening change – an assault on your 'security'. How can we immediately change with it?

Well, if you are a hundred per cent honest with yourself the relationship with your lady was dragging you down anyway and what's hurting you most is not so much your broken heart as your wounded pride. Now you are on your own again . . . time perhaps to start doing some of the things you have always gone on about doing but were never able to 'because you were married'.

Sacked? Terrible job anyhow. You hated your boss. And you hated yourself for going along like a lobotomized drone all those years. Now is your chance (remember?) to set up on your own at something; find a way to become self-employed so that never again will anyone be able to hold a gun at your head or chop you. It is the perfect moment to find the independence you have always yearned but were too afraid to try for.

The loss of the house? If you are honest again, it would have cost you more than you were able to afford and you would not for one moment have enjoyed the upheaval of having to move anyhow. On this occasion we are thrown off-balance not so much by change as by a thwarted desire-to-change, but of course this still means we shall have to rethink our lives to accommodate the change of plan! One cannot get away from it; the remorseless flux.

Your daughter's impending motherhood at the age of fourteen may at the outset appear a disaster *de luxe* for everyone, but ruthless appraisal will often reveal that what upsets us the parents in particular is not so much the prospect of the girl's future being jeopardized as the fact that her 'good name' (and more important perhaps, your own) has been cast in the mud, somewhat.

Should we still be concerned about the opinions of others and more to the point their prejudices and half-baked ideas in relation to the way we feel about ourselves and our hopes of happiness, we have a long way to go yet to find the latter, I am afraid. We can never be free inside if we are tied to mere social definitions of what is good and true and what isn't. Instead we end up as sheep (or worse, stormtroopers). So the only good name we should be concerned about in our quest is whether we have one in our own eyes when we come to scrutinize our consciences in the mirror.

If Mrs Batty down the road wishes to go around sounding off that in her estimable opinion your Deirdre is nought but a trollop, then Mrs B., needing to denigrate others in this way in order to try and find her own values and happiness in life, is clearly not having much success in her venture. So it does not assist our own if we immediately start feeling holier-than-thou and putting down Mrs Batty for putting down our Deirdre. We are only getting caught again in tangles. With awareness and compassion we ought to know better.

Still championing the Bright Side, Deirdre's having the baby may be a traumatic experience but we do not help her by tearing our hair out and ourselves making her feel like some strumpet, so if we are gracious and gentle with her in her hour of need we are likely to improve our relationship with her anyway, considerably, and she is then certain to gain some useful lessons about life and herself from the whole episode. Through our tenderness and humour D. may grow to love her precipitous motherhood, and make good of her life.

Getting up in arms about her predicament (or any other for that matter) is not going to help it one iota. On the other hand using it wisely, bending with the change, might transform everything into a story with a happy ending. A simple observation, some might say crass in its obviousness. But how many of us see what is obvious at the moment we most need to?

Yet you are still not wholly convinced by all this, maybe. 'Quality', 'Acceptance', 'Going with the flow', etc. – all these are wonderful concepts in themselves and no doubt they can all teach us something valuable about coping with many of the pitfalls we meet in life. Many.

But the very worst? Not merely disaster, but unmitigated horror? No – here, you are sorry, you finally 'pass'. There are some things too evil to be 'transformed' like this, either now or later.

Isn't it a bit preposterous to expect us to find something immediately 'positive' for godsake in, let us say, Deirdre's *murder*? Is it not straining credulity too far, to ask that we do?

To a large extent the reason we would find such an idea difficult to entertain is because we see tragedy in purely negative terms. Death, particularly. We are not much given these days to the idea that death might conceivably be a gateway to a mode of consciousness far more pleasant than anything we are used to in this existence. So we reel under the horror of Deirdre's exit, seeing it as the end of the world for our loved one and very largely the end of the world too for ourselves. All our 'security' has finally been shot to smithereens.

But as civilizations wiser than our own have perceived it, fortune and misfortune, happiness and unhappiness, are not fundamentally different from each other, they are merely the two sides of the same coin, which is life, and if we are to live this well we have to see the singular *importance* of tragedy to our enterprise. In itself it is not something 'hateful' at all. Only we, reacting, can be that.

As anyone knows who has ever watched tragedy performed well on stage or gone deeply into a great tragic novel, these can have such a cathartic effect on us that we leave the theatre or finally put down the book feeling strangely alive and happy! We feel we have been plugged into the very heart of life, that we have *lived to the full*.

We have. Tragedy purges, cleans us. It rids us of our pettinesses, confronts us with the Void, the fundamental emptiness of everything, the fact there is no security to be had anywhere – except in the way we relate to the fact. It leaves us with essentials. And we can only be happy when we know what these are.

Of course I shall weep over Deirdre's death. I'll feel distraught. Things will be much changed now, and her going will leave me, possibly, with lifelong ache. But I do not know that she has perished for ever nor that her death was not some instrument to her benefit and perhaps even my own. To see her demise as a full stop and accordingly to react with bitterness may be to do her a disservice. Wherever she may be now it could be that one's eventual equanimity, one's abiding love for the life she has left behind, can, in memory of her, do most for her.

If we are determined to take our revenge on life, to wreak havoc on it in hatred of what it has done to us, all the fancy phrases in her praise that might be carved into our daughter's gravestone cannot redeem the fact we cannot have known how to love her properly while she was alive, for such a love, being indivisible, could not now be divided by the circumstances of her death. Love, once born, can never die. It is only what masquerades as love in the service of self-interest that withers in adversity.

To hate Deirdre's murderer and wish to see him destroyed means that in certain (adverse) circumstances we ourselves could have learned to hate Deirdre and wish her dead, too. Thus we did not love her 'come what may'. To have loved her with the great love, I would have to share it with her murderer now.

Oh I shall want to grind his face in the hideousness of what he has done, rage at him until such time he begins to 'die a little to himself' and sees the wider implications of his action; that the murder of one human being is the murder, the further degradation, of us all.

I shall not in the conventional sense like him.

But for the sake of the love for my daughter and all men, among whom he is numbered, I would fight to save him from the hangman.

So even as I subside into grief as the enormity of my child's killing breaks over me and all meaning and purpose seem to shatter, there is still the love and the life that remain. There is that haunting possibility the dead child may be with me even now. Then, the loveliest thing I could do to remember her, I realize, is to turn her departure into the arrival henceforth in my own life of something especially beautiful – perhaps even a fresh life for others, or at least the vision of same. And as they bury the child in the good earth, to nourish new life there, I see that perhaps this is my greatest trial; that I have to let go of my loved one just as I must abandon everything else, piece by piece, in the quest for that which remains when all is lost. An ancient Greek proverb reminds us of the dogged route this, the last great journey, must follow: 'That which a man most loves shall in the end destroy him.'

In the name of that love, we must build by clinging to nothing, not even that love.

Chapter 15
Overcoming our own deaths

Of course what we hang on to even more than love, more than anything, is life itself. This attachment is said to be an instinct that helps preserve it. It is often, however, what is precisely the cause of its death.

Death itself, the great unknown, induces such fear in us it leads us to commit the most grievous errors in our lives that speed its arrival.

Having little or no idea what death will amount to, but for the most part foreseeing it as a bloody awful business in all probability, we, as they say, live our lives in its shadow. In such an environment it is not likely therefore that we shall come by much sun.

Death makes it difficult for us to abandon ourselves even to the good times when they do arrive. It is always hovering over there out of the corner of our eyes, mocking our gaiety. In bad times, 'death' in its inimitable fashion usually contrives of course to make them even worse. Altogether, a considerable obstacle it is to our happiness.

We try to overcome it, packing our lives with wealth, things, deeds, titles, honours, offspring and *How To Be Happy* books in the hope life will make sense in time; so death will not render it altogether futile. We note that we have only around three score years and ten to accomplish all this, so we must hurry.

And the more we pile up and the faster we go the more it seems we are finally going to be rubbished by death; find nothing.

But even if by and large we think we have done the right things on the journey so far (learned to make a banquet of beans on toast and see both sides of the question, etc.), all our accomplishments will come to nothing if we fail at the final and most difficult hurdle, which is the manner in which we come to our own extinction. We have to find a way to feel easy about this approach, so our terror of death will vanish.

Again, as with coping with misfortune, a conventional religious faith might be a help here since usually it would enable us to spy at least the possibility of a heavenly peace to follow and compensate us for our present less than illustrious existence. So long as we mind our Ps and Qs down here there is the *hope* anyhow of some future relief.

If we do not believe in God or have no feelings of certainty that there is an afterlife of some sort, however, adhering instead to the respectable contemporary emphasis on proofs not faiths, how in the face of a death which possibly offers only 'meaninglessness' do we find a meaning for living?

Why go on?

It would be valuable here to bring the open mind we have been trying to nurture all along to the problem of death. The latter offers us two broad scenarios. Either it is the end of everything or it is the start of something else. In the West, with our propensity for thinking we always have to make hard choices about things, of plumping for the 'either' or the 'or', we tend to split into two divisions on this issue as with any other.

If, however, we could again sit down quietly a moment and see that neither intellectual doubt nor religious faith proves a thing, that all we are blessed with basically are warring factions shouting 'Yah boo, sucks!' at each other, it may dawn on us that the most sensible thing to do perhaps is take a middle way and approach our deaths on the basis that they might be black-outs and they might not, and live *accordingly*.

If they are 'the end' there does not seem that much point huffing and puffing throughout lives like we do, trying to build fortunes and empires, trampling on one another and giving ourselves heart attacks in the process. A modicum of effort, yes, for the sake of future generations, to leave them something; but the sheer frenzy, heartache and all the useless things we come by – with it all ending in dust, what do we struggle like this *for*?

Should death be a beginning though, and this life be only one interlude on a long journey, we could well ask ourselves the very same startled question. With life stretching into unimaginable aeons, why all the *rush* to accomplish everything in a mere forty, fifty-five or seventy years? Why don't we ease off and enjoy life more . . . contemplating where this long, strange odyssey might be taking us? Why not *let go*?

Being open to either possibility, saving ourselves the necessity either of proofs or faiths, simply accepting the inevitability that death must amount to one or the other, offers us the opportunity then to take some of the pressure and tension out of our lives. The mad rush to get-and-spend and then get and spend some more becomes a pretty futile exercise whatever happens.

Now you may feel that the second proposition, life eternal, does offer a meaning or reason for this brief existence; if nothing else, out of a sense of curiosity, we wonder what will happen in the next incarnation, and what happened in those past; and above all, who or what is in charge of the whole mysterious process. But the first scenario, a finite allocation of years, may make it more difficult for us to answer the question 'Why go on?'

If these three score years and ten are such a headache usually, why bother to go through with them? Why not end them now, save ourselves more 'meaningless' hurt and confusion? What are we not only struggling for, what are we simply *living* for?

But throughout our search for happiness we have seen how important it is not to 'live for' anything, for some future event of goal, but to get on with the life we have now, which so far as we can see offers the only 'meaning' it is ever likely to have. So yes, if we think seventy years is a miserably short quota of breath and a pointless one to boot since it does not end up doing very much or going anywhere, then there does seem to be a reasonable case for jumping forthwith into the nearest river.

However, if this moment is 'what life is all about' and not what some Oxford professor tells us it is, or what tomorrow brings, we can with a little ready-reckoning see there are an awful lot of moments to be lived even in a span as relatively short as seventy years. So, why not enjoy to the full these moments we have?

The lives of the butterfly or water strider are 'miserably short' also, but within the dizzy, floppy career around the flowers or the high-speed darts along the skin of the water, among the breezes and the ripples and what seems to be a freedom (and a great deal of danger), one cannot help feeling there is an inherent order and beauty and not a few glad . . . moments.

Feeling better? Then go up another gear. If we are going to wind up as nothing, might that not be an almighty relief? Think of it; if we do have to go through Judgment Day and the possibility of million-year sentences in vats of boiling oil, or through the harrowing process of rebirth and going back to school, growing up once more with spots on our faces and girls laughing at our John Thomases, then recycling through divorce, redundancy, herpes, bankruptcy, suicidal inclinations, etc., etc. – is there not something to be said for annihilation after all?

On the other hand if this life is only a preparation for something else, so it becomes a constant assessment with exam finals to follow, it might give us something to aim for (if we will insist on aiming at things instead of being the bull's-eye ourselves), but it might not do very much for relaxation and spontaneity while we are about it. On the other hand again, if this is all we have, a life like a passing meteorite, acceptance of the possibility can spare us a lot of planning and worry.

You could say 'Fine', a nice way of dealing with the unknown in life; but it is not the living which worries me – I can make something of that, one way or another – it's the dying, the act, that does. Whether it is the last act or only one in a sequence, I am frightened by the entire process of death; the pain, disorientation and squalor it threatens. So while I can resign myself to what happens before and after dying, I cannot come to terms with the death itself. In that case I am still going to have this life blighted by the whole business. I can't win.

Death being such a nicely sanitized affair in the West these days, since we tend to find it 'disgusting' and shovel it out of sight and out of mind, very few of us become intimately acquainted with the subject until our own time is up. It is a nice paradox that our penchant for science, logic and tidiness, disciplines which cannot quite come to terms with death, should see to it that this should end up more of a *mystery* than ever.

Wiser preparation for dying would inform us that by no means does it have to be the obloquy of our night-time fears. It does not always come to pass as torture and sorrow. Death can arrive as something greatly welcomed, the falling of the ripe fruit from the tree; a life well lived but now worn out, its end encompassed with quiet relief. Here it is – the great and final act of 'letting go'.

The words of the dying on their deathbeds and of the mystics speak to us time and again of the exquisite pleasures and beauties that can accompany the leaving of the flesh. True, there can be some abominable experiences too if we have led equivalent lives, all the nightmares we have created for others and therefore for ourselves ganging up to haunt us in life's last, not so sweet revenge. But sometimes the scene is one of peace and beatitude, of a sense of floating and a vision of light. Incredible light.

Those who have been pronounced clinically dead but survived the ordeal, such as the victims of road accidents or heart attacks, have recounted vividly the unearthly radiance they have witnessed and, especially, the 'Being of Light' who has appeared before them in an out-of-body consciousness they have drifted into; a guiding force or spirit emanating powerful feelings of love, warmth and humour . . . and assuring the 'deceased', 'Everything's all right.' In case after case the experience has altered the survivor's life profoundly, imbuing it with a much more relaxed attitude, and spiritual strength. They have lost, altogether, their fear of death.

Ah, you say, determined to leave no corpse unturned, the actual passing away may go all right but what about the bit beforehand, the slow dying of the light in this life, perhaps over many months or even years, when mind and body might well be in a frightful state? What would happen if I were to find myself being eaten alive by cancer – and how can I tiptoe through the tulips in the present if one day I may have to endure something like this?

Once more, sentence of death itself does not have to be unmitigated misery; indeed it can make for great enhancement of life. Life lived to the full for once.

I used to know a distinguished cancer specialist who said he might have considered giving his work up if it had turned out to be a matter only of dealing with rotting flesh and vanquished hopes. Such might have given him neither reason for his labour nor faith in life. The pointlessness might have been too much for him; he would have been embittered and angry. What kept him, however, not just at his work but excitedly committed to it was the great beauty he was often able to witness rising out of the ravages of the disease.

There were instances, naturally, when people did not accept what was happening to them and were bitter about it to the end, but the surgeon said there were many other occasions when the announcement of 'only another year or two of life' did wonders for it. People were transformed out of all recognition. For the first time ever they gave up the struggle to live and just lived as though each breath might be the last. They did things they would not ordinarily have dreamed of. They dug into resources of energy they did not even know they had. Death staring them in the face, they were literally reborn.

'They glow with an inner light that's translucent almost,' the doctor told me. 'They exude such peace. And through them you see for the first time in your own life that *this*, this almost brutal recognition of the brevity of life and the sweetness such insight brings to each breath, is the only way to live; for all of us. Confronted by this degree of acceptance and grace in a person, I can only stand in awe. The power of disease and death is broken completely, and this brings rich new meaning to life.'

I also used to have a friend, an Indian journalist of refined sensibilities and rare powers, who forecast his own death within months. Since he was such a spirited, laughing creature, and not yet thirty, no one took a blind bit of notice of his daft prophecies. It was not until he was killed, on cue, in a Himalayan accident that I realized the undoubted connection between Pankaj's awful self-knowledge and the unforgettable luminosity of his character.

Death, cry the more formal prophets, the ones who tend to see our three score years and ten as a can of worms from beginning to end, is the great liberator from this life. Viewed however from a perspective even more detached than that, with the present seen to have a few things going for it as well, death can also be the great liberator *in* this life, whether we have any specific foreknowledge of our eclipse or not.

For if the idea of a sting is removed altogether from the tail-end of our lives then the whole course of ageing which begins the moment we are born is much less likely to alarm us. This freedom from fear will be all the more precious as we pass the meridian of our lives and begin to move at what invariably appears to be a gathering speed towards the end. Growing old will not come equipped with all the usual dread. Senility itself, should it come to that, is more likely to be a hazy inconvenience rather than a terror.

If we are not living in a constant quiet horror of things like grey hairs and colostomies we are much more likely to be able to enjoy the meridian years, and if in our youth we do not shiver at the thought of having to come to terms with a middle age of declining sexual vigour and promotion prospects (as youth, wisely, tends not to do) we shall be free to 'swing' with this the more. And so the long shadow of death dies itself.

Whenever that shadow does fall across our paths and life looks futile, to the extent we experience that it has already come to some sort of end, it is nearly always a help to be able to take ourselves off into the depths of the countryside and there to sit, breathe and watch. A day off from work, an excursion from the routine of home – take the car or a bus and 'lose' yourself completely. Cut off for the most part from Nature in our concrete boxes and one-track minds, we have lost contact with that which can most help us find ourselves and some pattern or purpose in our being here; lost sight of what is 'natural'.

Take with you these words on happiness by Joseph Addison:

> True happiness is of a retired nature, and an enemy to pomp and noise: it arises, in the first place, from the enjoyment of one's self ... it loves shade and solitude, and naturally haunts groves and fountains, fields and meadows: in short, it feels everything it wants within itself, and receives no addition from multitudes of witnesses and spectators.

Then, if we look at a wild flower, a particularly beautiful one, we reflect that it will only be a matter of days or a handful of weeks at most before it will have lived out its 'futile' existence and withered into a crispate ugliness. Really, what was the 'point' of that all too brief lifespan? What has it 'produced'? The sort of questions, you'll notice, we regularly ask ourselves when we are shot with doom.

Well, to begin with the flower may have given seed to others which will keep a cycle of beauty alive, and failing that, its own decomposition enriches the soil in which it has stood, to enhance the growth of ever more life of some kind. So either way the flower cannot be said to be wholly without purpose. Nor can it even be said to 'die'; something of itself is carried on to the future – cells, energy; a consciousness of one kind or another – even when this particular formation/force has expended itself. In Nature there is no such thing as a full stop. Everything must give rise to something else. Every one of our lives has value in the evolutionary matrix. Even the evil one enables us to define and know what is good.

But, you say, you want to know what value your own death has; what is the precise purpose of the set-up beforehand with its mortgage, delinquent teenage daughter, nodding-doggie in the back window of the car and nodding spouse in the simulated leopard-skin seat next to you? You can accept your rotting corpse might one day nourish a cluster of wood anemones that could lead a next-generation depressive to nod sagely over the value of rotting corpses, but you also want to believe this one small life itself has some intrinsic and higher value even whilst it proceeds.

Look again at the beautiful flower; a lone, totally defenceless, transient thing which 'does' what?

It makes you stop and look at it. It moves you. It inspires you (that is if you are not too obsessed with yourself). There is about it a touching vulnerability, an aesthetic beauty and a life-affirming sense of mystery (and where would we be without mystery? We would be bored stiff) which speak directly to such things in ourselves, because the flower *is* us. We are made of the same elements and share the same instinct to push our way up through the dark and reach for the sky. The flower confronts us with qualities in ourselves which tend to get lost in the daily grind but which we need to keep in touch with if we are to see life as anything more than that, as having some 'point'.

Then the flower, as does all Nature, has such associations with our poetic, artistic heritage that even if we are forced to live in a darkened cell, the flower, the waterfall, the sunrise and so on are by mere recollection able to act as a spell or charm, sufficient within the mind or upon the page to offer sustenance to our besieged resources. A very powerful electrical generator, then, is our tiny flower!

Ourselves, can we ask anything of our lives as they are lived more than that they likewise move and inspire others and enable them to generate within themselves an enjoyment, a meaning, in their days which lift these beyond their merely being a 'grind'? Can we achieve any good greater than that of giving others a practical demonstration that love and 'letting go' (things of beauty) are not the idle stuff of idealism and rhetoric; they actually work?

You may say the question still is not answered properly – what at the close of day is the 'point' of all this 'love and letting go etc.' if the world goes on being a place steeped in so much injustice, horror and pain; the rewards or what we usually understand to be 'rewards' invariably going to those who live by an unequivocal creed of lovelessness and grasping?

But here we confront the Unknown, and have to give way to silence. Before doing so, all one might say is that the truly good person does not concern himself with the popular notion of rewards but finds his own in the quiet happiness he is able to come by even in this life; a happiness he knows must communicate itself to others somewhere along the line and help them in their own search for it. Whatever might be the long-term resolution of this endless interplay of good and evil does not matter unduly; what does is the simple fact that right now in the daily round, 'good' makes life happier for most people. And that is enough, the nearest we can come, now, to making sense of the mystery.

Doing that is the task we impinged upon in the Prologue; the important one of each of us trying to make the world a slightly better, happier place for our being in it. When the task is multiplied, seen on a global scale, our being able to find individual happiness does not seem quite such a social irrelevance after all; indeed it could be *the* point or purpose of our lives.

Yes, yes, you might be getting carried along quite nicely by the argument and even be living with a pretty easygoing attitude to change and death right now, but even so there is a sneaking fear that remains. 'I may gladly accept even the fact I might die of cancer,' you could say, 'and see the possibility of being able to enjoy a very genuine love of life in any small portion that's left me. Except for one thing. If I didn't have twenty-four-hour access to drugs, say, how would I cope with the pain?'

A life of endless upheaval, nothing to hang on to anywhere throughout its duration and a death that may or may not be 'the end'; in other words nothing you would be tempted to describe as a salesman's delight – this and more we might decide we can handle. We could even see our way in the end to coming to terms with the cruel murder of someone we love. But, we wonder, would not all the linguistic finery about equanimity, peace, etc., turn to so much ash in the mouth the moment *we* got cut down by torment?

Is not pain – not your pretty metaphysical/mental kind, *angst*, alienation and all that, but the 'real thing', the searing, breathtaking gougings of the flesh – the point at which happiness collapses and all our philosophies, flowers and 'better worlds' with it?

When Christ was being nailed to his cross or the Gestapo were taking a man's fingernails out, could they the victims remotely be said to be 'happy'?

Is not this the juncture at which we are defeated, with our brief, the idea there can be such a thing as a happiness which is 'shockproof', in ruins at last?

I do not think so. There are many accounts, not a few contemporary, of individuals who have been able to withstand pain which by rights ought to have resulted in death through shock at least – and withstand it with spirit intact. Pain, as they say, is only in the mind, and this can accomplish feats even greater than the conquering of matter; it is capable of winning that ultimate victory, the one over itself. This strength has enabled human beings to opt for death in torture instead of betrayal, seen them recover from the most appalling accidents and illnesses, and given us those who can walk on flaming coals or pass blades through their flesh and smile. It has given us a fair number of our 'miracles'.

But perhaps miracles are not such uncommon phenomena

anyway, only part of the natural order of things. And when we respond to it 'naturally', perhaps terrible pain itself need be no more of an obstacle to our happiness than any other hiccup in our lives.

How, beyond the mere theory of it, do I know?

A small, illuminating experience. Years ago I suffered a run of bladder stones and when they got lodged in the urethra I would be felled in the street or wherever I happened to be by the sensation of having a red-hot poker stuck up my innards. I had two or three emergency admissions to hospital. Usually I got blessed, rapid attention in the form of a knock-out injection, but on one occasion I did not, I was left lying around a corridor on a trolley, barely able to believe what was happening to me.

At the best of times I have an abysmally low threshold to pain as to not a few other discomforts, and when one is abandoned to the full-scale experience of dying it is not an experience I myself come to with the best grace in the world. For a long time I lay and howled and thrashed like something on the rack, beating tattoos with my fists on every available surface. No one came to my assistance. I had never known anything like it.

Then, when it all got too much for me and I was not prepared to carry on with this kind of humiliation any longer ('To hell with it, all right, if I'm going to die, I'm going to die: so be it') – in other words at the point where I stopped struggling and gave way to the pain, let go, fact took over from theory and the body did its 'natural' work. Its pain-control system came into force, as it is said to do when it deems the time is right; the brain's pituitary gland producing substances called endorphins which have chemical structures similar in some ways to morphine and other opiate drugs. The result was the body-mind not only ceased to experience the slightest pain, it also floated off into the kind of candy-coloured realms, unutterably beautiful and voluptuously peaceful, you are only supposed to encounter on a good trip on LSD or magic mushrooms. Now I only wanted to lie there for ever. I was happy as a sandboy. Mothers who have known natural childbirth perhaps know what I am talking about, too.

By a mental process, a subconscious one of abandonment,

even torture was drawn of its sting. And when I realized the implications of this I began to see that henceforth there was not all that much to fear anywhere. Death itself approached in a similar frame of mind would have its own compensations, its own fantastic dream sequences just as real if not more so than anything experienced in this life . . . so long as we made sure the present was no nightmare; instead, the stuff of our dreams.

Heaven and hell were *not* so much locations on another plane of existence as the day-to-day realities of our minds in this one. And it was up to me to decide which I would rather inhabit; that is to say, which I would make a habit of living wherever possible, not in the 'next life', but now.

Who knows, clinical death might even be more than a tolerable or pleasing affair with helping hands from benevolent 'spirits', it could turn out to be something thoroughly exciting, and if we keep ourselves open to that kind of possibility there can be no doubt of the advantages to the way we live in the meantime. For example, there are documented accounts of the deaths of individuals who had reached such levels of spiritual refinement that their passings were undoubtedly extraordinary experiences. Allegedly able to transfer their consciousnesses to their next 'incarnations' as a yogic exercise, they dissolved their bodies into the elements so that barely a trace remained. In so doing they are said to pass into the 'Rainbow Body' or 'Body of Light'.

I have had a first-hand account of this happening in Tibet in the 1950s. A revered holy figure who had died was laid out in his monastery for the great farewell, lamas and monks gathering around. Slowly, the body began to decompose and contract. Over the passage of hours or a few days (I cannot recall the time-scale) the process accelerated. Smaller and smaller grew the corpse until it was reduced to the dimensions of a child and finally shrank, my witness said, to 'the size of a thumb'. Then as this dematerialized it gave rise to a blaze of gorgeous rose-coloured light that filled the room, investing the assembly with feelings, it was said, of 'great peace and joy'. The light hovered. Slowly it faded, and then was gone. The 'saint' had finally taken his leave.

It has to be admitted that the deaths of the majority of us are likely to be rather more mundane affairs than that with no doubt quite a degree of apprehension and pain of one sort or another being experienced on the way, especially as the end draws nigh. But so many mysteries surround our dying still, and there are so many accounts of the post-death experience which bear such striking similarities, in myth, religion and now medicine, all of them lifting tantalizing corners of the veils on these, the supreme mysteries, that to approach our surcease in an attitude other than of wonder is, surely, illogical? A certain trepidation, yes; such is understandable and probably natural. But resentments, loathing and fear? To do that is almost certainly to ensure that our deaths are as wretched as we foresaw – and made – them.

If we can 'let go' sufficiently to be able even to look forward to death in a curious sort of way – as an apparent resolution of an awful lot of our current predicaments at any rate! – our lives will be transformed so greatly we shall feel we have died and been reborn even in our present bodies.

It is death and our whole way of looking at it which is the key to life – to the only one that could truly be said to be worth the living.

Chapter 16
And flying high

As (if) we progress along the road to happiness and begin climbing towards its more rarefied heights, we shall find ourselves going through all kinds of 'little deaths', and possibly fairly rapid ones. Our past and its cravings start falling away at a quickening tempo, littering the wayside with the scrap of discarded dreams, and we feel lighter and lighter. We want much less. We are much happier to 'be'.

Most of us have had the pleasure of being able to go on holiday at some point and break with routine. Have you ever wondered what it is expressly about these vacations which makes them so attractive? Is it not the fact that everything we do and see appears new and fresh to us now, as though we are looking out at the world from an altered psychological perspective, or cleansed eyes? It isn't so much the sun, fun and sea air which are getting to us, it is the altered vision of life. It is the life where we let go and enjoy ourselves a bit, usually 'doing' very little.

Sunbathing, floating in the warm blue water; sitting on the quayside dangling your legs over the edge with a glass in your hand, not thinking about very much in particular – it's the nearest most of us get to sustained meditation these days. And which of us would not wish to extend through the other fifty weeks of the year the kind of feelings we get from it?

If, being of fairly sound mind, you have done any sitting meditation so far and kept it up fairly consistently, after about two, three months you will almost certainly be feeling 'different' about your life to quite a positive degree. You may, it is true, have found a lot of buried feelings, often negative ones, coming to the surface and upsetting you to some extent, and may even have seen your quiet twenty minutes and more sometimes interrupted by (if not disintegrating altogether in) tears. But for all the unsettling, perhaps even disorientating elements, generally you will have found that the peace and quiet you have been able to tap as well has enabled you to see the upsets for what they are and use them to understand yourself better. You have as it were performed your own catharsis and begun the process of what meditation is all about – self-healing, pure and simple.

We may not always understand what is happening to us in the course of it but the important thing, if we do become aware of improvements in our lives, is that we realize it works. At last we start to feel we are in some control of our lives. We have the power to change them. Here endeth the search either for scapegoats or saviours.

This is a supremely important milestone.

Once meditation has proved itself to your liking so it becomes a feature of your life, you see clearly how little you do need in these usually careworn years in order to experience happiness. If through self-help like this we can create feelings of warmth, compassion, peacefulness and humour, why all the palaver of having to subject ourselves to the usual mad scramble acquiring things, positions and accolades, and finding our 'highs' through the external and costly ministration of such as alcohol and drugs?

A spare half-hour perhaps, a cushion of some sort, and that is all we need to be able to set ourselves up for the day. One day we might not even need so much as that.

The full dawning of what all this means is more than a relief, it can amount to an experience of near-ecstasy in itself! All that money and grubbing; the weird dance of one step forward and two steps back, of trying desperately to belong to a system which amounts to a systematic violation of community – we can be spared nearly all of it. The time and effort we'll save; the knots and disappointments we'll be spared! The madness!

If meditation has begun to bring this kind of freedom to your life and it is something you would like to develop to a very fine art, it would be useful for a while at least to do your practice regularly, a couple of times a day. Your happiness is no longer something you're flirting with. Now, you are *committed*.

Half an hour (an hour even, if you fancy it) in the morning and fifteen minutes in the evening before you eat make for a positive schedule. Morning first thing, the moment you have awakened, is a lovely time for the exercise. Your mind has been swept clean by sleep (unless you have tossed and turned the night away in nightmares), your body is lissom, and there is an energy abroad in the world at that hour which is distinctly conducive to light and silence.

If this means you have to get up quite a bit earlier than usual, do not fret. Within a couple of weeks you are likely to have found you do not need so much sleep anyway, and the earlier reveille becomes no great dolour. After a time you may even find your sleep requirements are cut dramatically. Some people I have known, leading very busy lives, have with meditation been able to thrive (literally) on around five hours a night, and you should rarely need more than six to six and a half. Some folk have been known to cut right back, happily, to as few as three! So you should have little problem 'recouping' the time you spend meditating.

Your evening session, at home at the end of a working day, before you settle back to enjoy your date, the TV or whatever you have planned, acts as a pleasant transition from one to the other, often melting away the cares of work to a remarkable extent and providing you with a splendid second wind for the remainder of the day. Highly recommended. If you practise just before you go to bed, you may find it a struggle to stop yourself nodding off, which does not do very much for the exercise.

There might be other occasions such as your days off when you want to go even further, meditating perhaps for a couple of hours or more at a time. If you can get out into the country, settle yourself by a stream (the chatter of running water is a peerless aid in ridding one's mind of its own) or in a glade, or on a quiet stretch by pond or sea. The longer you can meditate, the more interesting things can become.

Once you are centred in your quietude your sense of time may go haywire. You are there, sunlight into which you have melted, and the minutes and hours may have no meaning any longer. You have no place to go, no wish to fulfil. You're content to be there and could remain so for ever. There is a great stillness and peace, and the sunlight, you may find, grows brighter and brighter.

When we speak of light in reference to such as character, meditation or spiritual considerations, it is often assumed we are dealing in metaphors, attempting to describe a quality in something. After all, there is probably no word more overworked in relation to matters spiritual than this one. But in fact we are not always setting out to convey a feeling only.

Once a person has delved deeply into himself in this way he does not necessarily merely feel 'light', 'pretend' he is seeing it. Sometimes, though by no means always, he might possess the faculty to see light as clearly – as 'real' – as if he was staring into an electric bulb. What begins as a visualization of the sun behind closed eyelids can in some individuals develop with practice, and whole-hearted commitment to a better life, into a generation of energy inside oneself, a physical heat, strangely attended by calm, measurable even by scientific instrumentation. And this energy is seen and felt by the meditator – rising like a fountain from the seat of one's emotions, the solar plexus, then pervading one's whole being – as soft light; gold or eventually some other colour, or white.

Do not be upset, feel you are 'inferior', if in all honesty you do not 'see' any light. It is not important. What is, is the tender feeling you allow to permeate through yourself. Meditation is all about 'heart', not magical light-shows.

As one sinks deeper into radiance whether 'real' or imagined, the sense of self as a person with a very clear outline sitting there doing some meditating is likely now to grow correspondingly weaker. Thoughts will come and go still, but you will not be anything like your usual slave self to them; they will have a lazy, almost languid quality, passing by like fish in an aquarium. You might now find the act of looking dispassionately at your thoughts quite entertaining. The way the mind tends normally to get swamped by them will in your new detachment even appear funny, possibly. All that fuss and nonsense which works us up into such a state all the time – and it is nothing other than the creation of these wayward minds!

At a very high level of meditation, about which you need not concern yourself at this point, the immersion in light will result in the meditator losing all sense of self. He *is* the light, utterly, and has no feeling of separation from it. It is not something inside him, it is something he has become.

Here he will seem altogether free of the body and its concerns. He will be streaming – at what feels like the speed of light – into space; literally, there may be sensations of falling or drifting through emptiness, but it will not be a queasy experience in the least. It will be a lovely weightless – care-less – one. One feels like a bird: one flies!

But long before we reach these contemplative summits, when we still have to shift our rumps and knees constantly to ease the stiffness, and worries about the overdraft continue to compete energetically with mystical transcendence, the light one has been able to visualize or experience perhaps a little more intimately can even here be felt to be working constructively on various planes.

It feels a bit like the fire that cleanses plague.

And we can get sufficiently rapt in it for even our own minds and bodies to want to stretch and purr.

Leaving aside its accomplishments for the moment, there is probably no finer indication of the power of that mental light as a simple phenomenon than our emerging from a lengthy meditation within a shady room or in an alfresco twilight. Opening your eyes, you will be astonished to see how dark your surroundings are. You had no idea! Up to now all you had been experiencing, or imagining, was a luminosity bright as a Mediterranean forenoon.

That there is electricity in the body, light, is of course a fact. That this light has a power transcending mere electrics is manifested by, among other things, the remarkable impact it can have in a person's eyes ('mirrors of the soul'); the fact that in the form of a halo it is the most prolific transcultural symbol of spiritual endowment; by the mystery to which it gives rise in the auras said to surround all life forms; and by such reported spectacles as death's 'Rainbow Bodies'. It is a light which obviously has a lot to do with the mysteries of falling in love and the attractions of making love. It is the light which comes off the healer's palms in waves of heat. The light which makes millions want merely to touch the robe of the likes of Pope John Paul. Clearly it is something to do with the spirit; the energy – the grace of God, pneuma, life force, subtile fluid; none of us truly knows what – at the heart of all life, the 'stuff of our being'. And therefore, what more precious? What more worthy of our awe, and study?

When our happiness is threatened direly, with life full of perplexing questions that never seem to get any nearer the answers, and voices bark at us 'Where's the proof?', 'What do you believe *in*?', and 'How do you *know*?', and certainty dissolves into silence, as eventually all certainty must so do, what is more logical than that we should follow where this leads us, and enter the silence too? And once we have done so and discovered something beautiful and nourishing in the light into which all questing, questions and answers, alleged sureties and all their come-uppances and final silencing would seem as a natural law to proceed, what could be more logical and natural both than that we devote our lives to that which illuminates them in the widest sense?

But while the act of sitting quietly as one (but by no means the only) way of exploring our inner treasures might appeal to you, the idea of visualizing things like the sun – that's taking matters a bit far you may think, entering the realms of hocus-pocus perhaps? Is not this merely using one's mind as a conjuring trick, which the good old masterminding, rational ethic finds distasteful?

The fact is, however, that visualization, much used once upon a time in prayer and meditation, does unlock powers within us which even scientists are taking an interest in these days, not least in the area of cancer treatment for example, where it has been shown that the contemplative visualization by patients of natural agents attacking the malignant cells in their bodies can actually work.

If a treatment for cancer can be had sometimes from creating pictures in one's mind, why not one for the blues? Mind over matter indeed.

We should not be nonplussed by all this. The power of our own mental images we can discern at a simple level every day of our lives. If we bring to mind the face of a loved one we feel appropriate feelings of warmth and affection. If we summon the memory of some ancient personal disaster, we may shudder still. The mind-picture of someone with custard pie over his face or her knicker elastic in ruins will invariably tempt a smile out of us. If our heads are full of gloomy scenarios all the time we do not expect to be other than thoroughly browned off.

And our sexual fantasies speak for themselves.

So why should mental images of benign light held steadily for reasonably long periods not increasingly imbue our whole lives with just that quality? It makes simple sense. If we polish anything long enough it shines. All we need is the will to see that we get down to the polishing. The rest follows naturally.

The polishing still does not have to be undertaken even now in the form of structured meditation. You need *never* get down on your backside and light your candle if you do not want to. Happiness will follow our days more naturally altogether if only we would not keep dividing them, and ourselves, into two apparently irreconcilable styles of life, the sacred and the profane; simply that. It is this division more than anything which causes us our unhappiness, and never more so than today. Having rejected the opiates of religion and found the opiates of its antidote, the popular satisfactions of the secular life, no more useful to our happiness, we no longer seem to know which way to go or what to do next. Have we not tried everything, and has not all of it been found to have holes in it?

If we look more carefully, however, we shall see we have in fact only rarely 'tried everything'. Usually we have struggled to be either one thing or the other, on the side of the gods or of proud, Promethean man – our tilt, you will recall, towards either life eternal or life 'full stop' – to the rigid exclusion, in nearly every situation, of the contrary perspective.

If we are rationalist free-thinkers and materialists we seem to need to back up what after all are only our own 'beliefs' by constantly inveighing against the opposition, deeming the spiritual experience to be hokum but in so doing denying ourselves any *possibility* of learning something from it.

Then if we subscribe to religious beliefs we have a habit of looking disparagingly upon the material world and its creeds, seeing them as the work of diabolic forces which can be guaranteed to prey upon any lapse in our spiritual vigilance, so the very flesh we stand up in itself presents a threat. This does not do a lot for 'joy in the moment' – give us much opportunity to be able to find something affirmative among the chores and teapots of our days.

Most of stand broadly in one or other of these camps. This only aggravates our unhappiness, since all of us possess both the sacred and profane in our make-ups, so that adhering overwhelmingly to one whilst trying to smother the other must therefore only worsen our hereditary split, when the purpose of human life would appear to be to mend it.

The unity we look for in ourselves will make redundant the idea of six days a week for 'sinning' and looking after Number One on earth, and one a week for repenting and hoping to look after Number One in heaven. Such division is typical of dualistic theologies, split personalities and hopelessly contradictory societies. Using churches or temples or indeed any fountain-head of spirituality in this way makes them a form of 'soul garage' where we go for 'repairs'. This suggests that our non-spiritual lives are forever breaking down. They do not sound very happy.

Happiness, by contrast, is about doing running repairs on ourselves every day of our lives – every moment in them – so they continue to run fairly smoothly through all contingencies. Our own bodies, our whole beings, are our churches and temples, and our only God or gods is this daily life.

Everything we do is 'holy'. The profane aspires to the sacred and the sacred finds itself in the profane. Psychologically we erase the barrier between the two. We live our lives according to that creed we have looked at in detail, Quality, knowing we can do no more and that in this knowledge lies the secret of our contentment; that when we die it will be enough that 'We've done our best'. If they must gild a stone with an epitaph, there will be none finer: *He/She tried.*

To learn how to love: we can do no more. And that is all we need to learn. All our knowledge and wisdom will come from there.

The dark side of life is likely to be with us always. We are all Auschwitz commandants, murderers and rapists. And all of us, too, are saints. So there will be choices we shall have to make all along. We are never likely to be allowed to *sit back* and be happy. Perhaps it is the fact we are not permitted to do so, the fact that choices are thrust upon us remorselessly, which grants us the possibility of coming to know a very real happiness – not some bland, paradisical, cow-like contentment which does not even know what it is because it has no dark side with which to compare and define itself, but a peace wrung from hell and high water that 'knows itself' because it is *earned*.

All of us have an idea of some perfect world, and many like to believe we inhabited one once, before our Fall. But if this Utopia ever did exist and there is a God who administered it, perhaps His allowing us to 'fall' was not the great misfortune we like to think of it as, but the most beautiful of His devisings. Up to this point, couched in perfection, we were nevertheless slaves of this God. He gave us no choices. As if in sleep – in ignorance – we did His (perfect) bidding. But in tearing all this up and setting us down in a world where there is evil and uncertainty, might not this have been His supreme compassionate act?

For in giving us the freedom of choice, He set us free. He enabled us to grow up, cease being His 'children'. And it is simply our free choice whether or not we mature.

Then, perchance we do make something perfect of this maturity; find love, truth and beauty in spite of all the impediments arrayed against them in this life; would not this be the crowning glory of God's work, the perfection of perfection, since we had found these things for ourselves and made ourselves in His image, instead of being merely 'made' in same?

If there is such a thing as a Grand Design, might it not be the fruitful outcome of the *partnership* of God and man?

None of us knows. Such questions are fascinating, and they might be an inspiration to some of us. But as the questions tie themselves in knots and inspiration fades, all comes back still to . . . silence.

What we do know is that when we have travelled the world over in search of the Holy Grail, ransacked the texts of the saints and sages for clues as to its whereabouts, pleaded with the night to yield it to us, abased ourselves in rituals, followed the light paths of romantic love and relationship and the dark ones of drugs and disorder, and *done* the million and one things it appears we have to do before finally we grind to a halt in exhaustion, our happiness still tantalizingly out of reach; then we see with a snort of absurdity that there is nowhere left to reach out to; that all the words have gone. The running, brother and sister, is done. The answer is contained here in this frail being in this dark night on this blasted heath; here or nowhere. The Holy Grail is *us*.

But we have not found it even now. In many ways, being within us, and our not knowing ourselves well at all, the prize is farther off than ever.

So begins the great dismantling of oneself. Plate by plate we remove the rusting armour. Our clothes we throw aside. The skin we peel off and the flesh we step out of. The bones fall away. What remains is the answer.

The teachings of ancient wisdom did so much for us. Layer by layer they disabused us of all ideas and concepts. The moment we thought we had 'got somewhere', they rearranged reality so we were made to see we had gone nowhere at all. Come up with even so much as the sniff of an 'answer' and it promptly vanished like smoke. Know a moment of happiness and you would be made to feel downright smug. Open your hand to give, and somehow it would contrive to snatch. Open your mouth to expound a profundity, it would dribble down your chin like spit. Take one step forward and, yes, be tumbled two steps back.

Write a book titled *How To Be Happy* – and O preposterous fool, glad fossicker, know then what it is to know nothing, and be sad!

Through the slow, systematic clearing out of all the lumber inside us, proceeding little death by little death until it seems (O terror!) we have nothing left, with all exits barred to us at the last and no succour to hand . . . so wisdom showed us what is this thing called life.

This breath, heartbeat and the love most of us have been able to feel at some point or other – these and the certainty of our perishing; there isn't a great deal more. There is our delight in the flower to feed on; the love, in the delicate perfection of its shape and colour, it seems to bear *us*. There are the sun, moon and stars to remind us of a power in the universe we can only approach in humility and wonder. All else is man-made contrivance and tangle. Guaranteed loss.

By this time we have well and truly torn the oppressor's 'clock', all his works, out of our being. Whatever society might do to us now, it does not matter. We are free. Free to care for a world which perhaps for a long time seemed to care not one whit for us. Turning disadvantage into advantage – that, it might be said, *is* what life's 'about'.

It may seem an arduous, even impossible road, all this, to follow; 'the path of saints'. 'Hell,' you grumble, 'I don't want to be a *saint*, I just want to be happy! If I might be arrogant enough to say so, I'm humble enough to know my limitations!'

To be happy, however, is in some ways to be more than a saint; a figure, faintly waxen, whom most of us would consider to be not quite of this world. To be happy according to our lights is to be a rounded individual who is very much 'of' it, who lives, dreams and suffers like everyone else yet still comes up smiling, a lesson and an inspiration to everyone, when the world chops him down. A man or woman who works long hours, has a mortgage quite likely and kids to look after; who maybe enjoys a drink, cigarette and a knees-up; and can still wander out into the back yard of a starry midnight and give thanks, with joy, for the fact he or she is alive. A person who is flawed, sometimes thrown by events, and in many ways terribly ordinary. A human being who even in this shoddy, unkempt age still aspires to the good, the better and the best; who does not go along with the shrugs and the 'Sod its' but sees the hope of our future invested in everything that is involved in the still unconquered impulse of *care*.

Meanwhile when it all gets too much for you and the 'care' seems to lead nowhere other than to ash and rejection, with the future of the whole world looking an odds-on bang or whimper, so all round the most sensible thing to do seems to be to stick one's head in a bag; instead, take yourself out into the backstreets or the park and have a good rage, hissing 'Dammit, I love you!' to the four corners of this obscene and glorious planet, and maybe shaking a fist at the (heathen) heavens while you are at it. Let the tears come if they must.

If you can still cry out 'I love you' in this long dark night of our soul and raise a tear on the rumpus, then, one hopes, follow it with a fair giggle at your Oscar-winning performance, you do not have much to worry about. You are not one of the robots.

You feel. You weep. You laugh. Tender shoots appearing out of the space and silence at the centre of your being beyond the frets, come the beginnings of the answers to all questions, the remedies for all ills: step by step your own small life, you vow, as gift.

Be glad, for thus you know what and how it is to be happy. Now go and toss this book in the wastebin, and *live*.